How I Started My
Home-Based Wholesale
Real Estate Business

My Journey To A Successful Real Estate Investing Career

by
Bobby Blair

Editor

Linda Pentz-Gunter was an editor and journalist for 20 years. She was an editor and reporter for *Tennis Week*, as well as a freelance writer for Reuters, *The Times* (UK) and other news outlets. She also served as a television commentator and interviewer for USA Network. In 1998 she shifted her focus to environmental advocacy and in 2007, founded Beyond Nuclear, an anti-nuclear environmental nonprofit just outside Washington, DC.

Executive Editor

James Forsythe has worked with Robert Blair since 2003 as his General Manager. In addition to being the office manager and overseeing all the working pieces of the power team, he has assisted Robert in writing, editing and presenting the educational material for Real Estate Investors. His technical and relational skills make him a valuable asset to the Turnkey Home Buyers USA roster of mentors.

Design
Dennis Dean
Ed Bosca

How I Started My
Home-Based Wholesale
Real Estate Business
by Bobby Blair

Copyright © 2016 by Bobby Blair
Real Estate Consulting USA / Publisher

ISBN-13: 978-1536870466 (Custom Universal)

ISBN-10: 1536870463

BISAC: Real Estate Investor Education

All rights reserved. No part of the book may be reproduced in any form by any electronic or mechanical means, including photocopying, recording, information storage and retrieval without permission in writing from the author.

Email:
Bobby@bobbyblair.com

Contents

About Contributors II
Dedication V
About Shane Hackett VII
Foreword Shane Hackett IX

Introduction: Take Action Today! 1

Chapter 1: My Early Years 3

Chapter 2: Building My Skill Sets 7

Chapter 3: Early Professional Life 11

Chapter 4: My Real Estate Start 19

Chapter 5: Where Are The Money Making Wholesale Properties? 25

Chapter 6: Funding Strategies That Made My Dreams Come True 31

Chapter 7: Matching Buyers With Property For Fast Profits 35

**Chapter 8: How I Mastered Renovating Affordably
Along With Creating Maximum Value** 41

Chapter 9: Renting and Selling Strategies That Turn Profits Into Reality . . 51

Chapter 10: How To Turn Your Network Into Your Future Net Worth 57

Chapter 11: Learn From My Mistakes 63

Chapter 12: Victories That Mean More To Me Than Any Profit I Earned . . 67

**Chapter 13: What Being A "Great American" Means To Me,
Will You Join Me?** 71

Epilogue 75
Robert Blair Acknowledgements 77
Statement by James Forsythe 79
Glossary 81

Dedicated to
my first Real Estate Coach Jac Klamper,
and my first funding partners Thomas Graham and Joe Roberts
who collectively believed in my real estate dream from day #1.

A special dedication to my mother,
Margaret Shields Blair,
who from the day I was born taught me to "DREAM BIG"
and always "GO FOR IT" in life. Thank you mother.

Thank you to "Success Magazine" for sharing my real estate career with the world and empowering me to help thousands of people learn from my experiences, techniques and strategies.

I want to thank you for taking the time to read my story. I am excited to be able to share my journey with you, and hope that by my sharing my life to realize my dreams will help you to dream big and achieve amazing successes.

If you commit yourself to your hopes and dreams, execute the strategies I detail in this book, then I know you will have a life well lived.

ABOUT

Shane Hackett

He is the Chairman of the Board and Partner at MarketLeverage. Market Leverage is a leader in integrated marketing. MarketLeverage has been an INC 100 Top Advertising and Marketing Firm and Fortune 5000 Fasting Growing Company.

He served as the President of PRM Media Direct. PRM Media Direct is the marketing arm for luxury real estate firms with over $2 billion in real estate assets.

Shane co-created the Success Magazine Conferences, training small business owners in all 50 states in management, marketing, real estate and sales.

He served as President and General Manager of the radio stations KGU-AM in Honolulu, Hawaii, KTSS-FM in Honolulu, Hawaii and WTIX-AM in New Orleans, Louisiana. He served as Director of Continuity and Executive Producer for Gannett with KCMO AM/FM and the Kansas City Chiefs Radio Network.

He has founded, sold and invested in several technology and training companies.

Mr. Hackett is responsible for the creation and production of several nationally syndicated radio shows, including "Baseball Sunday with Joe Garagiola," "Football Sunday" and "NBA Basketball Sunday."

Mr. Hackett is actively involved in multiple non profits. He is the Executive Director and board member of Heartland Soccer Association, board member of Kansas Youth Soccer, former President of Futura Futbol Club and Park Athletic Soccer Club, and is active building orphanages and designing and microfinancing projects in third world countries with Global Orphan Project. He is the Co-Founder of Life Giving Force and Life Giving Games.

Mr. Hackett graduated from William Jewell with Bachelor of Arts degrees in communication and public relations. Additionally, he studied international business and literature at Harlaxton College in Grantham, England. He currently sits on the President's Advisory Council at William Jewell.

Specialties: Integrated Marketing, Mobile Marketing, CPA Advertising Network, On-line & Direct Marketing, eCommerce, Web Design, Database Marketing, Social Media.

Foreword

BY SHANE HACKETT

I first met Robert when he became the face of real estate investing for the *Success Magazine* Conferences. We worked side-by-side delivering trainings and workshops all across the country. We bonded quickly, as we were both athletes who shared an entrepreneurial passion. Robert as a former tennis star and myself as a soccer player, we were now making our way in the business world. Our times together at *Success* were very fun and productive. Over $100 million in sales and training tens of thousands of people, it was an exciting time.

Anyone that has met Robert knows he is charismatic, upbeat, and a genuinely good person. He generously shares his energy and talents with others. Consistently at conference after conference, he channeled his charisma, motivating people to make positive life changes. It was really rewarding to be part of the process.

There is a common myth that successful multimillionaires never make mistakes nor have business failures. However, those of us who have dared start-ups to venture out on our own know that growing and running a business is not easy. It is not for the faint of heart. It is not a sprint; rather it is a marathon with a lot of twists and turns. If you look at Robert's track record of real estate investing, you will see his courage, and you will see success stories, some mediocre investments, and even some losses. It is precisely those years of varied experience — both good and bad — that make his story and his strategies so valuable. Because when it comes to real estate, it is just as important to know what not to do, as it is to know what to do.

What sets a winner apart is that he has the discipline to pull himself up and keep on going when times are tough. I have known many real estate investors and friends that were devastated both financially and emotionally during the 2008 market crash and recession, but despite the challenges, the good ones kept plowing forward. Call it commitment, persistence, or even sometimes stupidity, but the business is not over until you give up. Robert does not give up, and he can help you to stick it out too.

I have watched Robert over the years and learned from him. One of his true strength's is his ability to embrace change. If something is not working, he is quick to look at it and change it. In addition, he is not easily satisfied, so even when things are working, he looks at them, as well, to see if they can be improved. This search for continuous improvement has always served him well in his business ventures.

There are definitely cycles in the marketplace. There are ups, and there are downs. Despite where we are in the cycle, Robert has proven that he has the ability to cast a vision, identify where the market is headed, and develop a strategy for how to profit from it. At times the right strategy is to buy, fix, and hold single-family houses; other times it is commercial property. The key is to know which strategy matches the current market conditions.

In contrast to growing up as a soccer player, which is a team-based sport, Robert grew up a nationally ranked tennis player. If he was having an off game as a single athlete, there was no one else to help pick up the slack. It was all up to him. I have always wondered if that is the genesis for the great self-belief Robert exhibits. It is that same self-belief that enables him to excel as a business leader. If you have not yet heard Robert speak, you are missing out, not only on the inspirational stories of him learning to achieve but also on the transfer of knowledge from his long real estate investing career.

I am sure that you have heard the expression "Is the glass half full or half empty?" Well, Robert is a full-glass visionary. He believes in abundance, and he makes it happen. He did not come from a wealthy family; in fact, it was quite the opposite. He did not graduate from college, but he lives 'The American Dream.' I know that his infectious 'can do' attitude is a big part of his success, and a beautiful belief he holds is that others can succeed too. For Robert, it is not, "Hey, look at me." Instead, it is, "Here is what I have learned. I am happy to share my story with you, so you can benefit."

Most people simply are not good listeners. Their brains are running so fast; they want to talk rather than listen but not Robert. He learned a big life lesson growing up at Nick Bollettieri's' Tennis Academy. He learned what most successful athletes know; coaches can teach us what we do not know. In tennis, Robert learned professional skills from one of the most famous and best tennis coaches of all time. When he retired from tennis, he again used coaches to learn the art of real estate investing. Those friends, mentors, and coaches changed his financial life. With the expertise they taught him, he achieved success without previous experience and using none of his own money.

While there are actual strategies for investing in real estate such as buy, fix, and sell or buy, fix, and flip, mindset and attitude are also very important. Robert has always been highly motivated. He 'walks the walk'. He lives what he preaches from the stage and what he writes in his books. Having the self-motivated, winner mindset has propelled him forward, even when the odds were against him, and he can use it to propel you too.

In a recent video shoot, Robert was talking about several recently purchased properties and the corresponding strategies. One of his team said, "Make sure he doesn't sell too much." However that is the thing; successful entrepreneurs never stop selling, and they never stop closing. On an episode of *Shark Tank*, I heard Mark Cuban state one of my beliefs, "Sales cures all problems." While of course, the statement is an exaggeration; it does convey a very important business truth. If you have sales, you have time to work on the other business issues. If you do not have sales, you do not have a business. If I had to guess, I would say that is why Robert is always selling, always closing.

One of Robert's most endearing qualities is his desire to help others. In his speaking engagements across the country or working with investors one-on-one, Robert shares his knowledge, his stories, his experiences, and his strategies. He shares what has made him the successful investor that he is today.

Through the years, Robert and I have continued to be friends and business associates, and we have had time to reflect on our experiences – both good and bad. We are all on a path of self-discovery, acceptance, and celebration. For some, the journey is easier than it is for others, but for all, there is great meaning in finding yourself. Enjoy the book, and may Robert's life stories and strategies bring you closer to your own truth and financial independence.

Shane Hackett
Chairman of the Board
MarketLeverage

Introduction
Take Action Today!

Greetings,

If you have this book in your hands, you and I share a couple important traits. The first is that we see the field of real estate as the best pathway to improving our financial lives. We have concluded that real estate was one of the safest and most lucrative fields ambitious investors can pursue, and we wanted in.

More importantly though, if you are reading my book, it's because we share what I consider the most important personal trait to becoming successful, which is a dream big attitude.

Every successful person I've met was a dreamer, every successful venture I've embarked upon began with a dream. Before I found real estate, I spent my youth pursuing a professional athletic career. When that dream career did not fully materialize, the dreamer in me remained. Within hours of playing my last professional match, I was already creating my next opportunity, devising a new system for young tennis professionals like me to have more successful careers.

It has been my ability to identify needs and opportunities in all sorts of unique marketplaces that has been my strongest asset in my business life, an asset I plan to share with you in this book.

In the chapters to follow are some of the events and stories that make up my life, as well as quite a bit of my real estate investing advice. I share with you my upbringing, through my pursuit of a professional tennis career, to my first real estate deal, to some of the successes and failures in my career as a real estate investor, to show you how all my early life experiences prepared me to become a successful investor.

I will show you that you do not have to be born into great wealth to become successful, that regardless of our circumstances growing up, we have far more similarities than differences. All that is required is a dream big attitude combined with the desire to learn and apply the real estate investor skill sets I am about to present.

What I have found in my career is that smart financial resources always find a great deal. It's my objective here to teach you all the skills necessary to make your team extremely attractive to investors with resources. I will teach you how to locate them, how to wow them with your expertise, all the while helping you build a power team around you. I have been fortunate to have built many lasting win-win business relationships in my career. I want to share with you how you can build the same kind of winning relationships.

The skill sets I apply today I had to learn from the school of hard knocks. From a two-bedroom home in a rough neighborhood, to being the poorest kid on the tennis courts, to starting my businesses without a college degree or any funding whatsoever, I learned how to create opportunities for myself and others by learning and watching other successful men and women. Their success inspired me to step out of my own comfort zone and just take action with a "CAN DO ATTITUDE, NO MATTER WHAT."

If you want to fulfill your financial dreams for you and your loved ones, then I invite you to join with me as we journey together through the life lessons I learned that enabled me to generate millions of dollars in revenue in the real estate business. I have been blessed with a happy, healthy and fulfilling life where every day I jump out of bed excited to tackle the day ahead. I want you to share with me in dreaming big and having the courage to step out of your comfort zone on your way to financial success.

My mentor and friend Billie Jean King says "Go For It." I'm betting my book will change your life. My promise is this: everything you will read as you turn these pages is exactly what I believe and exactly what I do every day of my life. I started from ZERO, with no resources, just like many of you are as well. Join me today and lets do something special together. Let us move on this moment and make it happen.

Chapter One
My Early Years

With every success story, there was a beginning.

My family didn't come from much. We grew up in suburban Orlando in a small house on a dirt road. My dad struggled finding consistent work. My mom would pick up odd jobs to help make ends meet. We always had a roof over our heads, but there were times we had to forgo things young families should not have to forgo.

My mom was the family rock, teaching my brother and me the importance of faith, discipline and a work ethic to envy. My father was quite the opposite. He struggled to be a source of consistent support. I'm not sure which parent influenced me more; my mom showing me the proper ways to live, or my father showing me what I did not want to become. What I do know is everybody around us had more than us. I was too young to understand why they did, but I recall quite early in my life promising myself I was going to climb higher than what I grew up around.

My world view was limited at that time, my neighborhood being pretty much all I knew. I was a young kid dying to put my heart and soul into something. And, luckily for me, my mother found just the thing. She took a sudden liking to tennis. We were growing up in the right place at the right time; Florida in the mid-1970s, just when the world tennis boom was hitting. Soon my mother began taking my brother and me to the park to play tennis on a daily basis.

That first time led to a second time, and now it's been a lifetime. I was blessed with great athletic DNA for the sport, helping me pick it up quickly. My mom understood at the beginning that if I was going to keep improving, I was going to need some instruction and a place to play. She took a couple of odd jobs to pay for a junior tennis membership for me down at the local club. Now I had a place to play, at least for a little while. I was as excited as a kid could be to have the chance to make something of himself; and now it was up to me to take advantage of my opportunity.

My first few days at the club were unsettling. If I thought everyone in my neighborhood had more than us, the kids at my club took that to a whole new level. Everyone dressed sharp, had better equipment, their parents drove luxury cars, and everyone's home seemed like a mansion compared to where I lived. It was during those first few weeks at my club that my desire for a more affluent lifestyle really took form. I still had little idea how people achieved such levels of success; I just knew I wanted it and was willing to do whatever it took.

I quickly learned that nobody was going to just hand me success or wealth; I was going to have to apply myself to the fullest. But I did notice that there were people at my club that were very generous with their time and resources. Not having much, I could tell I was going to need some help to reach my goal of being a professional athlete. I knew intuitively, even then, how important it was to be likable and attractive so that people would take an interest in me.

Thinking back, I could have picked a more attainable dream. I could have picked one that wasn't going to take 10 years of my childhood and much of my young adulthood to see it through. But all that aside, I loved what I was doing, and it was that love that kept my dream alive. Because it wasn't always fun, lots of ups, lots of downs. But rarely was it not rewarding; every experience becoming a learning one.

My tennis journey taught me a lot; to take pride in myself, my talents, my physical conditioning. I learned it was acceptable to pat myself on the back a little when I achieved good things, that it was alright to feel good about myself. I was achieving success in a highly competitive sport, and I was learning that the real accomplishment was not in seeing my name in lights after conquering the world. The real accomplishment was becoming the best player I could be with the God given talent I had. Those lessons stayed with me throughout my business life too. And that's a lesson I want to share with you.

I had important people around helping me toward realizing my dream, none more so than my late mother. After I started to have some success, she could tell that sticking with the tennis was going to be my ticket to a better life. She took it upon herself to keep me focused by never letting me let go of my dream.

We had a little ritual we used to do. Our tennis club was near the Orlando Airport. After practice mom would take a detour from going straight home so we could have a little private time together. We had this place we parked near the runway where we could watch all the planes take off. I was intrigued by planes, but had never been on one. Mom used to watch the planes rise up during lift-off and say to me, "Bobby, if you keep working at your tennis, soon enough you'll be on a plane like that traveling all over the world to compete." All I can remember thinking was how much I hoped she was right.

And it turned out she was.

A "Dream Big" and "Go For It" attitude was nurtured by my mother and she would be proud of me today. My brother Joe (right) works with me today. His extensive knowledge of real estate and passion to help others is incredible. I know our students and clients are in the best hands possible when Joe is their mentor.

I went on to have a pretty decent career. Though I never became a superstar, I became a super player. By the time I finished high school, I was one of the top five players in the United States. I received a full athletic scholarship to play tennis at the University of Arkansas. From there I was asked to represent the United States in the Goodwill Games held in Russia in 1986. Professionally, I had my share of successes, defeating three future top ten players in the world, with a marquee victory over Wimbledon champion Pat Cash. Not bad for a kid who started with nothing but a dream and a never-say-die attitude.

My career started with a dream, a dream that was supported by several important people who I will introduce to you in the pages to come. As I said before, you are reading these words because we share the dream of becoming successful investors, but nobody can do it all by themselves. Allow me to support you as you pursue your dreams here with me.

Chapter Two
Building My Skill Sets

Part of my success story in becoming a prosperous real estate investor was my ability to attract partners with financial resources. I learned at the start that the most essential step in drawing investment resources toward me was to make myself attractive. Nobody was going to invest in me if I did not invest in myself first. On many levels, this was pure common sense. If I was hiring a trainer and had two choices to select from, the one well groomed and fit would be the obvious selection over the one not so well put together. Investment capital operates in much the same way. Investors have options. It's our responsibility to make ourselves the best looking option we can.

I was fortunate to experience the importance of this vital life lesson very early in my youth. My first real exposure to wealth and success came at my tennis club. As I mentioned, everybody there had more than my family and I and they were not shy about displaying it. One of those areas was in getting tennis instruction from the coaches at my club.

Private tennis lessons were expensive. Players didn't just take one lesson; they needed them every week for years. Obviously, my family couldn't afford any of that stuff when I started playing. What was available to me though, were the free group workouts the club gave for the membership kids.

At that time, and I was pretty young, I thought the tennis coaches at my club were the coolest guys ever. All I wanted to do was grow up and be one. I did everything I could to get their attention. What I noticed in those beginning group workouts was that the coaches paid considerably more attention to the kids who tried the hardest, had the most upbeat positive attitudes, who never complained, and always helped out when things needed getting done.

So I adapted. I saw what worked and altered my behavior. Class after class, I made it my mission to be the hardest working kid with the best attitude you've ever seen. Soon, the coaches began to take notice. As I continued to make the best impression I could, I started improving substantially right before their eyes. One of the coaches, impressed by how hard I was trying, rewarded my work ethic by offering to give me a couple of private lessons a week, free of charge.

I believe I was all of 12 years old at the time, but the life lesson was already clear. People will invest in me if I present myself as an attractive investment. I would soon learn later that the assistance I got was not entirely altruistic. The tennis industry was experiencing a huge boom around the time I started playing. Coaches could benefit enormously discovering the next great player. That's when I began to understand the importance of win-win relationships. If I were to hit it big, my success would be just as lucrative for my coach as for me.

The free lessons did just that. My improvement was immediate and dramatic. Before long, I was having success in tournaments, making a name for myself on the national level. The equipment companies soon took notice, wanting me to use their rackets and wear their clothes. They had choices as to who would represent their products. Liking the way I carried myself on a tennis court, the equipment companies decided they wanted the hard working kid with the great attitude to showcase their products.

As I continued to improve, financial offers of support began to come my way. A doctor from my club offered to undertake all my training expenses in exchange for a percentage of my career earnings. Not having much, this was tempting as could be. Yet, I almost threw it all away.

Not accustomed to my new found success, like a lot of kids my age, I allowed it go to my head. I began to act like the entitled kid nobody would want anything to do with. I started acting like people owed me something, that I was hot stuff, that now that I was so good, I could act any way I pleased.

In reality, I was a little uncomfortable in my skin, being the poor kid

This picture was taken just after my match playing for the #1 U.S. National Junior Tennis Ranking in 1983. I was learning how great coaching for me and hard work could create amazing results. My coach, Hall of Fame inductee Nick Bollettieri (center) and former top ten player in the world, Aaron Krickstein (right).

doing well at this rich kids game. I started acting all cocky, loud, and temperamental. I began behaving the exact opposite of what had been working for me.

Fortunately, my coach at that time was more than just a coach, he was my mentor. He saw the changes in my behavior, compelling him to write me a tough love letter well before its time. He basically said that I was becoming the kind of kid people weren't going to want around anymore, let alone invest in. The message was clear. Get back to being the attractive young kid I was before I blew my opportunity.

And I did. I soon signed the lifetime contract with the doctor from my club. He saw to it that I moved to Bradenton to train with Hall of Fame coach Nick Bollettieri. Once Nick saw the terms of my lifetime contract, he ripped it up, offering me a full scholarship to train at his Academy. He wanted to be my coach in case I hit it big. Two years later, the United States Tennis Association came calling, asking me to represent the USA internationally in Junior Davis Cup as well as at the Goodwill Games. When it came time to attend college, the University of Arkansas in Fayetteville, an elite division one institution, awarded me with a four-year full scholarship.

The list goes on. I point out all these situations because all of these parties had choices as to who to invest in and support. I was an amateur during all of this; there were no television appearances or huge paychecks to cash. My supporters kept picking me over my equally deserving peers because they saw in me the qualities they wanted to be associated with. It was a win-win before there were ever any winnings.

I'm certain now I attracted so much support because I made it a priority to make myself attractive to those with resources to invest. It was not just me either. There were also two great women players at my club, Nancy Reed and Mary Ann Plante, who were able to travel the world playing tennis tournaments. I remember thinking how in the world could they afford to do that?

Then I found out. They renovated and rented out homes for a living. I recall being so intrigued by a line of work that allowed people the freedom to live the life they always wanted to live. I was still a young kid, but the real estate seed had been planted.

In the next chapter I want to show you how my first three professional businesses, which had nothing to do with the real estate investment world — as a tennis coach, a professional World Team Tennis general manager, and a tennis academy founder and owner — prepared me for a real estate career that started at 27 years old and has allowed many of my lifetime dreams to come true.

Chapter Three
Early Professional Life

I retired from professional tennis in 1988 at the age of 23. For kids growing up where I came from, pursuing a career in tennis was just not done, yet I always had this drive within me to stand out from the crowd, to be the kid who came from nothing excelling at this rich people's sport. I put everything I had into becoming the best tennis player I could be. Though retiring from my athletic dream short of my goals was hard, I was able to walk away with my head held high and with few regrets. I knew it was time to get on with my adult life.

Now what? With no college degree and woefully short on cash, I needed to find an income and tennis was all I knew. I still loved the game and wanted to stay involved. The traditional, safe career transition for someone of my caliber was to go into private coaching, getting a job working for a club as an assistant professional while growing some roots in a community. There was nothing wrong with that choice, especially for the peers of mine who were tired of all the travel. But I wasn't quite ready for that life. I had other ideas about what my role would be in the industry.

In my years of competing, I saw that those who had resources had a distinct competitive advantage over those who did not. Though I personally was able to secure financing to help subsidize my travel and training, it was always sporadic and lacking in the long-term planning that would have given me the best chance at success. I knew there had to be a better way for young players like me to turn professional and be able to stay out on the tour longer. I just hadn't figured it out yet.

With tennis coach and mentor to this day Nick Bollettieri in 2014.
He taught me to think out of the box and that winning at every level in every way matters.

Hours after my last professional match, I was sitting at the hotel bar with one of my closest friends, taking inventory of my career. We both agreed the one area that would have made a difference in my career would have been some source of consistent support. Life on the road was just too expensive. Then the idea came to me in a flash. What if I were to arrange a professional tennis traveling team structured so it would give the next generation of players like me the best opportunity at the success I wished I'd had.

Before the end of that evening, the Rookie Pro Team was born, an organization that I would head as the primary coach, organizer, and fund raiser. I would essentially do everything for my small team of players, with my compensation coming from a percentage of their winnings, allowing them the best conditions to train together, travel together, all the while supporting each other as they pursued their tennis dreams.

It almost seemed too easy; we could not believe nobody else had thought of it. Within a month, I was able to parlay my connections in the sport with my reputation for being an upstanding hard working guy. At the age of 23, I had six of the best newly turned professional players just out of college signed to contracts with my new business. By just keeping my eyes open and being willing to try something unique, I was able to develop a creative way for young college tennis players to turn professional. The concept was strong with all kinds of room for growth if it proved successful. Now it was a matter of execution.

As the founder of a new organization, I wore all the hats in my operation. The tennis coaching part came pretty naturally for me, the rest I was going to have to learn quickly. Fortunately I was blessed with great coaches and leaders in my tennis experience, people I was able to emulate and draw from when a skill was required. Coaches and leaders like Nick Bollettieri, Tom Pucci, Ron Hightower, Mike Estep, Jim Kelaher; all successful people in the tennis industry in different ways, all of whom had something unique to teach me. Knowing how to motivate, to be organized, show leadership, and be a great communicator, while also learning how to become a fundraiser, was a lot for a 23-year old. Fortunately I learned from these men not to be afraid to ask questions about matters I did not know.

Ultimately, being the founder of the Rookie Pro Team made me the tennis coach to half a dozen very talented young Americans. Within a couple of years of working under me, six of them ended up playing in the US Open. One of my players would play a feature night match against the legendary Andre Agassi, while another player of mine would win the mixed doubles title. All their successes created a lot of buzz around me and my Rookie Pro Team concept, eventually landing me a high profile national sit-down interview on USA Network during prime time.

In the tennis industry, coaches are judged by the successes of their players. My guys were killing it, and I was getting a lot of the credit. From our shared success, I was able to leapfrog over a huge segment of the stay-at-home coaching industry, guys who were equally capable of coaching that level of players. The difference between me and them was that they lacked the vision to be different and stand out from the crowd. As you read through my story, think about the times you manufactured ways to stand out in your own lives. And if you have not, what forces have kept you from trying? Stay with me here on this journey and I am going to show you how to do just that.

How was I able to be so successful at 23 with no business experience at all? Simply, I applied all the traits I'm laying out for you here. What I did to be a successful coach are the same things I did to become a successful real estate investor. Making myself attractive to clients and people with resources; dreaming big, executing bigger, great work ethic, due diligence, being organized, having a plan. Life skills I learned on my way up that I plan to share with you here in my book.

Most importantly for my success, I was willing to take a chance, to dream big, that the success of the venture was not so much in the end results but in the effort, in the willingness to think outside the box and go for it when the opportunity presented itself. I didn't have to do anything overly special. I just practiced all the life lessons I learned as an up-and-coming player. When a venture is entirely yours, with your name and reputation on the line every day, it takes the work right out of the job. I loved what I was doing and what it was doing for me. But I also knew to maintain my elevated status in the tennis world, results mattered. People want to be associated with winners. Winning does matter. Always has, always will.

All that aside, I really wasn't making any money on the whole deal. After three productive yet exhausting years, the governing body of American Tennis, the USTA, co-opted my ideas into their own system, I was not terribly disappointed. I was getting lots of accolades and recognition that my idea was a game changer for the sport of tennis. The USTA would in time reward me with a prestigious offer to coach within their elite system of national development, one of the highest accomplishments a private coach can attain. I came home to Orlando proud about what I had been able to accomplish in such a short time, eager to find the next challenge.

My first business in the books, what had I learned from it all? I learned how to identify opportunities in a marketplace that had a need. Even at 23 and in a billion dollar industry with all sorts of major players involved, I was able to spot areas I could make my mark in. I learned how to put a spotlight on my best qualities; my work ethic and my dream big attitude, and get people to believe in me and my visions. Most importantly, I learned how to take a dream and make it a reality, by just implementing who I was and what I believed in.

Back home in Orlando, I couldn't wait to sink my teeth into my next venture. I believed I could succeed in any marketplace now. All I needed was the next challenge to conquer. That next venture would be the Bobby Blair Tennis Academy.

After all the years of travel, laying down some roots in a community sounded real good. Again, I could have easily stepped in to a safe teaching pro position at a club, where I worked for somebody else, but I knew better. Working for somebody else put me on the wrong side of the dollar. I wanted to be in control of my financial destiny, with my power team of expert tennis people working with me and for me.

To start a tennis academy, all I had to do was staff it, find a location for it, and cross my fingers that on opening day, the kids would come. With virtually no investment, I was able to package my brand as one of the young up-and-coming coaches in America to clubs in my area. This was the ultimate win-win situation. I was the local boy who had gone away and done good. Now I was coming home to help create the next generation of young Bobby Blairs. The offers from clubs to host my academy started coming in from all directions, and we had not been open for a business a single day yet!

As with any venture, there was always some risk involved. Helping mitigate my risk was having my best friend and assistant with the Rookie Pro Team, Randy Koehnke, by my side. We had worked great as a team together before; understanding the importance of having a trustworthy power team around me, I felt confident our great working chemistry would continue. We did everything we could to recruit as many young tennis players to attend my first day of camp. But until they arrived, we had nothing. On our opening day, I sat in the parking lot of the club, nervous as all could be that nobody was going to show up. But sure enough, the first car entered, followed by another, and another, and The Bobby Blair Tennis Academy was up and running and open for business.

The business got off to a great start, kids coming from everywhere to learn with me and my power team. It was an exciting time; all these kids and parents wanting what I had. Soon the kids were winning matches all over the place; and nothing is better for any business than winning. Winning matters, it's contagious. Once I secured my first deal and got paid, it was no different than winning a big tennis match...my confidence skyrocketed. I couldn't wait to do my next one, and my next one.

With success came some growing pains. My Academy was off and running and making a name for itself. Soon lucrative offers began to come in from even more high profile clubs in ever wealthier Florida enclaves like Wellington and Palm Beach. It would have been easy to stay put; I was doing good work and enjoying having a home base for the first time in a while. But the entrepreneur in me knew there were better opportunities out there.

Though I was implementing my long-term planning and cultivating important strategic partnerships, it was important to be flexible to changing market conditions. I call it "tweaking the dream." Entrepreneurs have to be flexible. Situations change, people change, market conditions can change, and sometimes conditions are static, other times quite fluid. We can't be afraid to adjust on the fly as conditions merit.

Even though moving my academy around was a bit unsettling, my status in the Florida tennis community was skyrocketing in the process. I felt it was just a matter of time before all my hard work and preparation met the opportunity of a lifetime. Then the call came in that took my tennis professional life to the ultimate level. I was asked to be a general manager and head coach of a World Team Tennis franchise. What an honor, to be the youngest coach/GM in League history at the time.

There are some people in life who are impossible to say no to. Billie Jean King is one of them. In the tennis industry, she has few equals, but her influence does not end there. Billie Jean has left a mark on late 20th century society that will last forever. So when I answered the phone with Billie Jean on the other end, asking me if I would be interested in becoming a general manager to one of her World Team Tennis franchises in Tampa, I jumped at the chance.

Did I know anything about being a GM? Of course not. Was I willing to do whatever it took to learn? Absolutely. Billie Jean sought me out over dozens of equally qualified peers because I shared the entrepreneurial acumen she possessed. She had heard about my go for it attitude with the Rookie Pro Team and my Academy and wanted to see if I was the right fit for her World Team Tennis project.

And I'm proud to say I was. Billie Jean taught me so much about busi-

Billie Jean King and I at the 2014 U.S. Open Tennis Championships. We shared time together at my book signing, celebrating a lifetime of mentoring and support towards me to a crowd of thousands.

ness; I would not be where I am today without that relationship. She taught me about persistence; about how to be aggressive, yet respectful, always with an eye on getting what we want and how we want it, that a "No" for an answer could always become a "Yes" if pursued properly and intelligently.

Billie Jean taught me the invaluable marketing lesson of under promising yet over delivering, something that has been a challenge for me my whole business life. As you can see, I get very excited about my projects and passions. I want people to share my levels of enthusiasm. Billie Jean taught me to how to "wow" people with results and not hype, that way the next business "pitch" requires far less sizzle. My greatest strength has come back to bite me sometimes over the years. I still work on that part of my presentation daily. But I believe in my heart that no matter what the endeavor, no passion means no results. The art is to manage the passion.

So there it all is. My three tennis businesses that had me on the cover of a *World Tennis* magazine special edition, asking, "Will Bobby Blair be the next Nick Bollettieri?" As much as I loved the accolades and success I was achieving, I still knew there was more out there for me.

I share all this with you because I want you to know some things about me. I didn't come from money, I do not have a college education, I spent the first half of my life with little knowledge of what real estate investing really was. Yet, when the opportunity presented itself to me, little did I know I had been preparing for it all along.

My belief is the life lessons I've learned will be quite similar to yours. You know a lot, you've experienced a lot. It's my goal to help bring your experiences to the forefront of your mind, help you organize them, see where you are strongest, see where you need help, and give you the boost you need to apply what you already know as you pursue your investing financial dreams.

But enough about me. Let's start talking some real estate. Let me explain to you how it all went down in my first deal in our next chapter.

Chapter Four
My Real Estate Start

The tennis business was good, life was good. I was doing what I loved the most, yet something inside me yearned for more. I was working ridiculous hours, driving at the crack of dawn from my home in Orlando to Tampa to work with the Tampa Bay Action WTT franchise, then returning back to Orlando on my lunch break to run my tennis academy all afternoon. I was still young and loving it, but I knew I couldn't keep this pace up forever. Then my opportunity for a better life appeared.

Enter Jac Klamper, real estate investing specialist. Jac's son was attending my tennis academy. One day after our workout, Jac approached me, saying he had something he wanted to discuss.

The crux of the conversation I would summarize like this: "Teach my kid to be great at tennis, and I'll teach you how to make a fortune in real estate."

Perfect. I had been watching Jac for some time come and go from my club. He had the kind independent lifestyle of wealth and abundance I wanted. And now he was offering me an opportunity to have that lifestyle myself. My learning curve could not begin soon enough.

Over the course of the next month, Jac explained to me all the different ways a guy like me could get into real estate. But what he was explaining to me was more than just how to do a real estate deal. He outlined for me how to go into business for myself in the field of real estate. He knew I wasn't an investor or a realtor. He just felt there was a place for me in his field of expertise, which was flipping houses. Flipping was the purchasing of distressed properties, and then renovating them with the intent to resell them for a profit.

Jac explained to me how the flipping market worked, who all the different parties were and what their specialties were. I want to stress I knew very little about real estate investing at the time I started talking to Jac. But it was not long before I began to see how the real estate industry set up perfectly with who I was.

Jac explained the flipping process to me, mapping out in detail the six stages to executing a deal. They are:

Find,
Evaluate,
Buy,
Renovate,
Market,
Sell or Rent.

It didn't take me long to figure out that was way too much for any one person to do by themselves. But it was achievable if I was able to assemble a power team of professionals who were up to conquering the task.

Let me explain to you how I was able to organize my power team around me to assist in orchestrating my first deal in real estate. Let me reiterate that my goal here is to teach you how to do the same; to start your own real estate business. This is not about teaching you how to do a quick deal to make a quick buck. I will be teaching you all the aspects of the industry so that you too can achieve the wealth and abundance about which you have always dreamed. Remember, every long journey begins with a first step. Here is how I took my first step in the real estate industry.

First things first, I had to find a property.

> **1) Find...** As it turned out, my mentor Jac was an acquisition specialist who understood distressed real estate markets. Jac had a keen eye for a special type of property called fixer-uppers, homes we could buy, clean, renovate, add value to, and sell for a profit. I go into much greater detail in the next chapter on how to locate such properties. There are people in the real estate industry who

specialize in just that; finding properties for investors. In time you will learn a great deal about this aspect of the industry. Until then, you will need to find your own version of my mentor Jac. They are out there, in your community, in your network, at your real estate investment clubs.

Jac was able to find me a property in the Tangelo Park area of Orlando, a modest first time buyer type of neighborhood perfect for someone like me just getting started.

2) **Evaluate...** Part of Jac's expertise was also the Evaluation process. This is where knowing the market comes in to play. How much to pay, how much for repairs and closing costs, how much value could we add, did the deal make sense to make? Much of that was determined by our investment strategy. What did we want to do with this property? Flip it? Rent it? Jac saw the Tangelo property as one we could fix up quickly, add value to, and sell for a nice profit all around. It was going to need some work, but nothing too dramatic. A lot of evaluating comes down to simple math and having some experience for what the local market will bear. As a real estate investor, Jac showed me that the spread was to be a profitable one for me. If our renovations came in on time and on budget, we would be able to add value to the property to turn a nice profit. This is where having a trusted and capable contractor on our team will be so important.

3) **Buy...** Once Jac explained to me the particulars of the Tangelo property, my next step was to secure funding. Enter Thomas Graham. After consulting with Jac and my contracting team, I knew funds were needed to buy and renovate the property. As I stated from the beginning, smart money always finds a good deal. My purpose here in this book and in my other educational tools will be to show you how to showcase your power team such that investor capital will know you have all your bases covered. That is my job, to teach you how to do this just like I learned.

In Chapter 6 I explain in great detail the power of Other People's

Money in getting started in the real estate industry. It's important for that first deal to secure a hard money- lender, as I did in Tom Graham. In buying distressed properties, securing a traditional loan from a bank is not applicable for two reasons. First, properties in need of renovations are not insurable for the banks. Second, banks do not like to loan money for the renovations to a property. Hence, we need to locate a hard money-lender who can be our point person for all necessary expenses.

I already knew Tom, having taught his son Matthew at my academy. I was doing good work for him; I knew he liked and trusted me. What I needed to do was trust in myself and my team to ask him to become an investor in our project. I laid out the details, the costs, and the timeline. We agreed on a 50-50 split of the profits. One thing I want to stress when you approach investors. Investing is what investors do. They need people like us to bring them good deals, trust me, they see enough bad ones. Without quality investments, their money sits idly on the sideline.

Once Tom Graham saw I had all my ducks in a row and he knew we would be able to execute, then it was just a matter of getting him to sign on the dotted line. An invaluable lesson from my first deal is do not be afraid to leverage your personal relationships. People not only like working with people they like and know and trust, they like helping people they like and know and trust. Make these relationships work for you. I made Tom Graham a lot of money and people found out about it. Before I knew it, everybody wanted in. When you apply my real estate investing techniques as laid out in this book, I hope your success will elicit the same type of response from your inner circle.

4) **Renovation...** Before there were any profit checks to split up, there was still some very important renovation work to be done on our fixer-upper. In chapter 8, I have dedicated a good amount of space teaching you how to renovate affordably and correctly. I turned out to be quite fortunate in this area as my father and brother were both excellent renovators, providing my investment partner and I

trusted competent contractors to use on our project.

I was lucky, I had family members who were in the rehab business. If you do not have family members in this field, you will likely have a lot of questions regarding renovations. What I hope will happen for you is that you will have in your expanding real estate investing network numerous experienced contractors that are in your local area. Ask around. You would never hire an electrician or a plumber without checking numerous references first; it should be no different when deciding upon a contractor to be a part of your power team.

A quick tip. If you are having trouble getting quality referrals in this area, call the most successful property management firm in your area. Tell them you are looking for a small renovation crew. Find out who they use for cosmetic repairs on their rental properties.

5) **Market...** Renovations are done, now it is time to put our property on the market. This process is far more involved than just sticking a sign up in the front yard. Remember, time is money. We want to get in and out as fast as we can. In chapter 9, I go into more extensive detail about how to rent or sell your newly renovated property. The marketing and selling processes are closely intertwined. The difference is the marketing is done solely by us to attract a buyer, whereas the selling involves having a skilled realtor at your disposal to close out your deals and make you the most profit possible. As it pertained to my first deal on the Tangelo property, Jac, my acquisition specialist, was also my realtor. Having a person like a Jac on your power team is indispensable, but don't forget, people like Jac need people like us willing to arrange the financing and improvements of these properties in order to bring them to market. As I learned very early, nobody can do solo. Everybody has his or her own expertise. It is people like us who are willing to do the work to bring all the talent together on a fixer-upper project who are so necessary for the functioning of the distressed real estate market. If you are to make money in real estate, you will need to have a solid power team of professionals.

6) Sell/Rent... Chapter 9 is dedicated to teaching you how to rent or sell your home. Everybody knows a realtor, likely a dozen if we think about it. If you had your own home to sell now, how many realtor friends of yours would want the listing? Likely quite a few. What is important is to understand the type of market we are dealing with and find a seller best suited for navigating that space. We each have our own best niche. Make sure you coordinate your buyers and sellers to the markets they represent. You need a sales specialist who understands the first-time home buyer market as well as the local and federal FHA down payment assistance programs.

And there you have it. This is how I started making money in real estate. And you can too. This is where our dream big attitude can become reality. We can't be afraid to leverage our personal relationships into the most advantageous win-win dynamics. Sell yourself, sell your team, sell your vision, and smart investor resources will find you.

It worked for me. With no cash investment I was able to build a power team around me that was attractive to investment capital. After word got around about the money that was made on my first deal, the members at my club were lining up to get in on the action. Within a matter of months, I was opening up my first real estate office at my club. It was such an exciting time with my clients coming by all day and night checking in on the progress of their deals.

Within a year, I was able to afford my own beautiful home with a pool, a brand new BMW in the driveway, and a whole bunch of cash in the bank waiting to be invested.

Thank you Thomas Graham for believing in me. And thank you Jac Klamper for seeing the right stuff in me to be successful in real estate. May you find in the following pages the same inspiration I did on my way to wealth and abundance as a real estate investor. And may you find the same information I did, the time-tested strategies and techniques for you to build wealth for the type of retirement dreams are made of.

Chapter Five
Where Are The Money Making Wholesale Properties?

As real estate investors, by the time we see the "For Sale" sign, it's too late. Someone else has reached the property owner and has been entrusted with finding a buyer. The topic of this chapter is how can you locate great properties with profit potential and have your name be the one on that sign.

On one level, the real estate business can be pretty simple. It all comes down to leads. Leads lead to business. Every marketing analyst would agree with this. The challenge for all real estate investors is how to get the best leads.

For me personally, I had great success with my mentor Jac, who was an expert acquisition specialist, but who also understood all the moving pieces to buying, renovating and reselling homes successfully. Jac was instrumental in helping guide me as I built my power team. Now that you are in business, you want to have strong working relationships with as many Jac's as possible. As I stated earlier, no one person can assume all of the duties in the fixer-upper space; people have their specialties. Acquisition specialists need people like you who can see the value in a property, secure funding, make timely renovations, get the property to market, and get it sold quickly. It becomes simple math. The more deals you do, the more profit everybody makes.

Just as you will know multiple acquisition specialists in the field, they also will know numerous entrepreneurs like your eager to invest. What is critical to your success is you need to be the first person your acquisition specialist thinks of when they get a lead. How do you assure that? By paying the best and by making timely decisions. Put yourself in their shoes. You find a property and you have a dozen prospective buyers. Who are you going to call first? You're going to call the one that pays you the best. You are going to call the person you know will say yes, rather than asking for a few days to think it over. You need to be that person. If you are not that person to your acquisition specialist, you need to find out what it takes to become that person.

Another way you can reach homeowners before the "For Sale" sign goes up is through direct mail strategies. During the recent economic downturn, many families experienced immediate and severe economic distress. Our national conversation turned to toxic mortgages, subprime lending, credit bubbles, and foreclosure rates. It became an epidemic, with all these first time buyers getting into their dream homes, only to see their dreams become nightmares as the economy plunged. If the changing market conditions were not affecting you directly, you didn't have to look too far to locate someone they were. The fear of credit ruining bankruptcies and foreclosures filled the air as homeowners calculated exit strategies from their properties.

Those troubled times are not over for many homeowners. But how do you find homeowners? One way to reach them is through direct mail. Two areas I encourage you to focus your direct mail strategy plan are pre-foreclosures and bankruptcies. You can search for these properties through county websites, and most search engines. You might also speak to a bankruptcy lawyer. Often they are looking for ways to help their clients who are struggling financially. A good relationship with a bankruptcy attorney can lead to a win-win-win situation.

http://www.realtytrac.com/ allows you to search any state and any county for pre-foreclosures and Lis Pendens. It is a subscription service, but could be a worthwhile investment in your business. You can perform a Google search looking for foreclosure properties.

Once you have located potential homeowners looking for a way out of their dilemma, you need to reach out to them.

Another area to which to focus our direct mailing are probate lists. Homeowners pass away, often leaving their property to be divided amongst

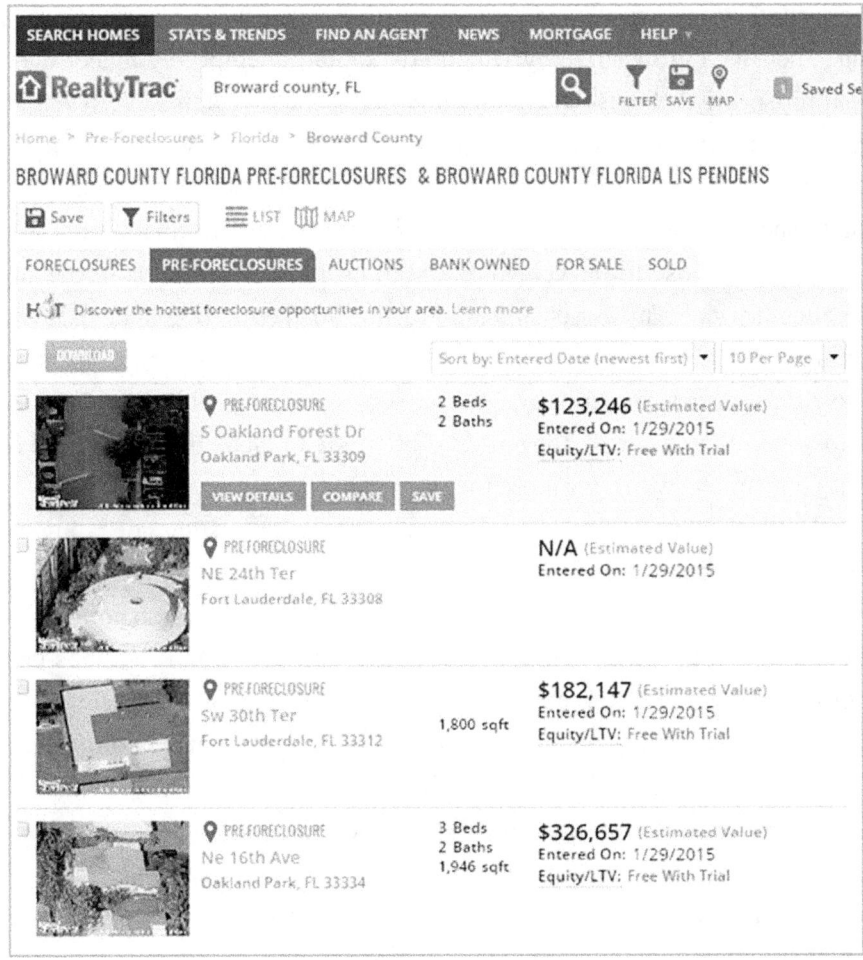

the heirs. Often these probate cases end in liquidations of all major assets.

Again, a well-crafted direct mail can be the deciding factor if they sell at all, and in particular, allow you to be the broker of their transaction.

A word of caution. Be smart here. The wrong tone in your message and a potential client is lost. We do not send the same mailing to everyone; it's crucial to craft a message specifically to your target audience. Do not be afraid to invest some money in this area. This is a very cheap method that can turn in to sizable profits if done professionally and properly.

There are direct mailing companies that will do this work for you if you have that in your budget. The science of a successful direct mail campaign is the response rate. Again, use yourself as a source of experience.

How much "junk" mail have we got over the years? It can be overwhelming. There is a proper rate by which you should attempt to connect with your prospective clients. Direct mailing firms should be able to help you in getting a positive response rate. This is about exposure. Even if recipients are not ready to pull the trigger quite yet on selling their home, you have established yourself as someone who will buy when their time is right.

If you choose to do your direct mailing in house, Microsoft has an excellent service. But be sensitive to the time you are putting in here. If it's taking you hours on end to craft and mail your messages, strongly consider outsourcing this work. You can pay someone around ten dollars an hour to help you with this; I will hope after a little time in the real estate business that your time is worth far more than minimum wage.

Another vehicle I like to use is signage. As the 60s song goes…Signs, signs, everywhere a sign.

Signs are a cheap and simple way to get your brand out into your community. Think about it. Every entity from politicians to corporations use signs of all sizes to reach their constituencies. Everyone is advertising who they are and what they're selling. Signage has become a huge part of every horizon we look upon. Most of the signage we cross we barely acknowledge at all. Ask yourself though. How do you know who the major players are in your area? What catches your eye, even for a quick second? Our goal with signage is to enhance your visibility. With visibility will come leads. Follow these pointers to enhance your visibility in your community

Signs are about awareness: that your services are available in the local marketplace. We live in a fast-paced world. People don't have time to read a story. Quick, bold, direct. "Quick cash". "We buy". "Sell your house now". If someone is considering selling their property, it's your signage that can tip their decision in your favor. It's your signage that will get the phone calls coming in, it's your signage that will start developing leads that will lead to deals.

Again, reflect on your own community. Which signs catch your eye? Is it the message? The design? The colors? The location? Likely it is a combination of all those factors. Assess what works best on you and do your best to replicate that winning combination in your signage.

As the old real estate saying goes, location, location, location. It is no different with your signage. Where you put your signs is critical to their effectiveness. But before you get all excited to go post 500 signs all throughout your community, you must educate yourselves. There are rules and standards for signage in your local community, otherwise it would be total chaos. Before you start putting your signs up everywhere, make sure you check with local ordinances.

You can always post your signs with your friends and your family. Homeowners proudly allow politicians to post on their lawns. Don't be afraid to ask your inner circle if it's alright for you to post on their lawns too. Just make sure you tell them it's not forever. If you have an active renovation site, be sure to post all throughout it. Renovation sites draw a lot of attention from passersby. Be sure when they glance over that it is your sign they see.

Finding other locations is mere common sense. Busy intersections and parking lots, especially ones of the major home improvement chains or high volume grocery stores are always winners.

As you are just starting out, this is an area where at first, it's best to post your signage yourself. A side benefit to posting your own signs is that you get to see the area. Many a great deal has been found by simply driving by and noticing a house that might be in distress. More on that later. As you get the hang of where you like to be seen, over time, there will be better ways for you to be spending your time. As your time becomes increasingly scarce, look again to outsourcing this work locally. Make sure to give whoever you hire a good tutorial on how and where you prefer your signage displayed. Again, make sure that to whoever you outsource this function understands the local ordinances. I don't want you overdoing it and getting yourself fined before you even start.

Post flyers in grocery stores, laundromats and any place that has community bulletin boards. Let people know that you not only buy houses, but sale and rent houses as well. Remember, the goal here is to create leads so that when you are ready to rent or flip a house, you have buyers.

Another vital way to generate leads is through old fashioned networking. Locate the local real estate investment clubs in your area. Here's a tip I want to share with you. In the beginning it's far more important to be a good listener than have a good pitch. The best way to see what type of delivery is most effective is to listen to others. Let them put their pitch to you.

See what you like, see what you don't, and implement the best techniques in to your own pitch.

Let people talk and see where you might be able to help them. This is how strong long-term business relationships form. Do somebody right, and they will likely do right by you. Don't feel like you need to blow everybody away right when you meet them. You all want the same things; find ways to work together instead of against each other. Make the people in your network colleagues and not competitors. It's worked for me, I know it will work for you.

In today's world of technology, the Internet is an important tool for you as an investor. Not only might you find a good deal, but sites like Zillow.com will help you see and understand market value. Google homes for sale in your area, check out Craigslist, look at sites like Yahoo real estate. Many homeowners needing to get out of their mortgages find that it is easier and cheaper to post on the Internet rather than place an ad in the local paper.

Last but not least is the MLS...the Multiple Listing Service....this is the bible for all realtors. It is the service that all realtors use to list and sell properties. Deals are harder to find here, as realtors will be listing their properties at or near full market value. Additionally, every agent and investor client has access to the same listings you will, making finding that under-valued listing all that much more challenging.

That said, it's not impossible. If nothing else, it is a great way to educate yourself about all the neighborhoods in your community, to know the asking prices, the selling prices, which communities are hot, which are not.

Depending on where you live and your local market, learning how to find profitable deals takes time. I used to look at 100 houses to pick the one to make the best profit from. But none of this happens without having leads. Work hard at this. Without leads there is no business. Establish your message and constantly refine it. You will never not need leads. Through amassing leads you will be able to locate great properties with excellent profit potential. And that's how we start making money as real estate investors.

A Contract for Sale for any state can be found through a Google search or from a local Realtor. At the workshop or working one-on-one with your coach, we will explain how to fill out the contract and what stipulations you will need to ad to limit your risks.

Chapter Six
Funding Strategies That Made My Dreams Come True

Other People's Money — it's a term we've all heard. It was the title of a Danny DeVito comedy from the 1990s. It's also the title of a famous book on banking a century ago. But what exactly is it? Other People's Money, or OPM, is what makes our economy function. It can range from our credit card purchases, to the loans on our cars and homes, to the corporate bonds that finance business expansion, to the federal government borrowing money to pay its bills. Almost all financial transactions in today's business world gets done with Other People's Money.

OPM does two important things for investors like us. If the market is favorable, meaning there are homes available that you and your power team could transform in to a profit, using OPM allows us incredible opportunities. It is a simple process of math; the more homes you're working, the more profit you can make.

For fixer-upper projects, you can expand your business dramatically if you are able to attract a type of OPM called a hard moneylender. Hard moneylenders are investor types who finance properties that most traditional banks will not lend on. Furthermore, hard moneylenders will loan you the additional funds needed to cover the renovation costs. Frequently, the hard money lenders I've encountered were former renovators themselves. They understand your investing niche.

Hard money lenders will charge higher rates and more points than a traditional bank. But that is not your concern. Often in our industry it is not the cost of money but the availability that is most important. You must calculate the cost of money into your deals. With your loans often in the 6-12 month duration, the higher rates still leave ample room for profit if you execute your repairs on time and are able to bring the property to market and make the sale in a timely manner. Once in business, with a growing resume of successful renovations and repayment of notes on time, you will be able to negotiate more favorable terms with your hard money lenders. Remember, smart money will find a strong investment. You start making money for the members of your team and deals are going to start finding you.

There are several places to look for hard money lenders. In your real estate networks, through Google searches, Craig's List, searching in your local community for this type of lender, or by asking around. They are out there as they play an important role in this vital sector of real estate investing. Find out who they are, get to know them, and remember, investors need a consistent stream of good investment opportunities to keep their profits coming. Make it your priority to have your team be part of that stream.

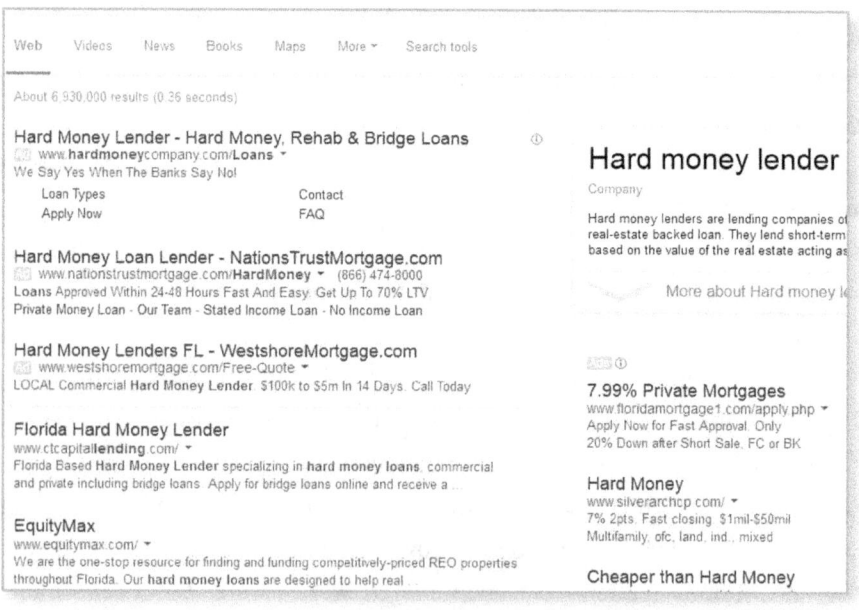

Google search for hard money lenders

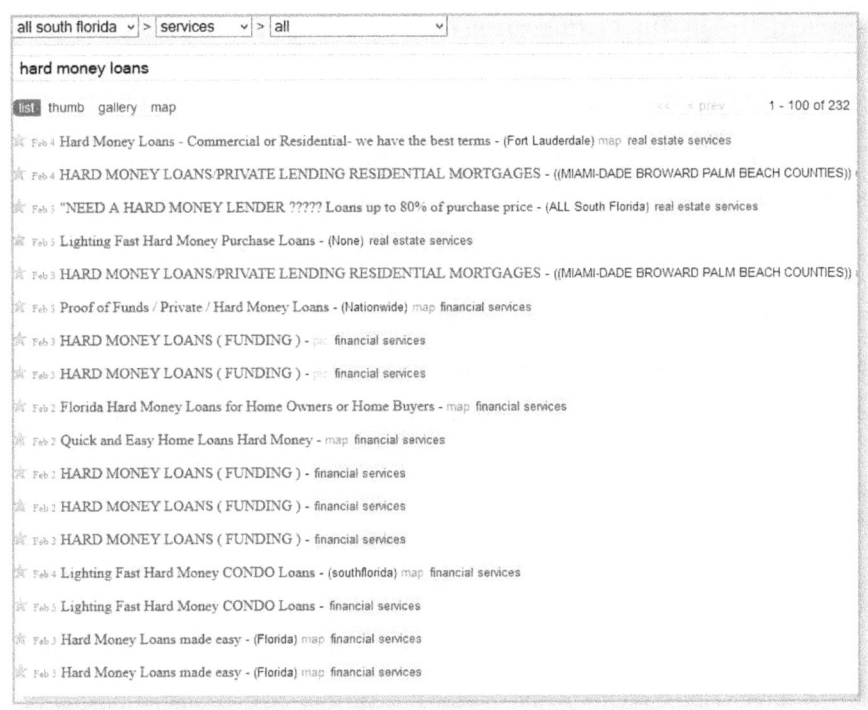

Craigslist.org search for hard money lenders under "services"

Once I discovered the power and availability of OPM, I realized I could do more than just one deal at a time. I could now utilize my partner Thomas Graham's resources to create more profit centers. We were able to simultaneously do multiple deals by bringing in hard money lenders to finance the purchasing price, or as much of the purchase price as possible, and using Tom's capital for the balance of my costs, closing costs, renovating expenses and monthly debt service to the first mortgage hard money lender until the house was sold for a profit. By the way, this is when it is important to have an efficient power team. Trying to do a single deal all by yourself is difficult, multiple deals would be almost impossible.

My deals amounted to a 50-50 split of the profits with my investing partners. Your breakdowns may be more favorable, or slightly less favorable. Either way, do not get greedy. You are partnering with OPM. These arrangements are mutually beneficial and should be the beginning of long-term and highly profitable business relationships. Don't sell yourself short. The work you are providing to attract OPM is just as important as the investment capital. Both parties need each other and you deserve abundance just as much as anybody.

At the workshops you will see a deal package I did with OPM, a hard money lender, to show you how all the price points break down in any given deal. This is how I did it. Behind all the math and details, everything I explain to you here still comes back to having the right attitude, that you too deserve wealth and abundance, that you too can dream big and make yourself into the most successful real estate investor. You're going in to business now. This is now what you do. Do it right, and do it with passion and you too can create the future you've always dreamed you should have.

> **Do I actually have to have money to make money in real estate?**
> **No!**

Chapter Seven
Matching Buyers With Property For Fast Profits

Up until now, I have been explaining how to locate, evaluate, finance, renovate, market and sell/rent a property. Now I will show you how, with minimal funds, another way to make money in real estate with virtually no risk to you. Welcome to the world of wholesaling.

You have located a property and have done your due diligence. You believe the property is a good deal. As a real estate investor, what you need to do next is to determine your exit strategy.

Once you have decided to buy and flip the property, you have two options. The first I have already explained to you in detail; the rehab. A second option is to wholesale the property. Wholesaling is either selling the contract (an assignment) you have written to purchase the home to another buyer, or close on the property and reselling it immediately to another investor.

Why would we want to immediately sell something we spent so much time researching and that may have even more upside profit potential if we were to hold and renovate it?

The immediate benefit to wholesaling is how quickly deals can happen. Rehab and larger development projects take time, where unforeseen issues can occur. In wholesaling, you can be turning a profit in as little as two weeks or less, and be done and free to move on to the next project.

Once you get good at finding deals, you may have more opportunities than you can rehab or finance. But, that is not a good reason to walk away from a deal. You can still make money by controlling the contract and wholesaling the property. Wholesaling is also a great way to generate working capital for the projects that you decide to keep for yourself.

ASSIGNMENT

1. The parties to this assignment are:
   Assignor: TURNKEY HOME BUYERS, LLC AND OR ASSIGNS
   Assignee: _____

2. The following property and/or right(s) to the property is/are the subject to this Assignment:
   Property Address Parcel #: _____ /
   LEGAL DESCRIPTION: _____
   City, State, Zip: _____

3. Assignor, Assigns and Transfers the foregoing property and/or right(s) to the property, and Assignee accepts the same and gives the following as consideration to the Assignor.
   $ _____

4. The Assignor acknowledges receipt of the foregoing consideration from the Assignee and accepts the adequacy and sufficiency thereof.

5. The Assignor represents states and warrants the following with respect to title or legal right the Assignor has to the property and/or right(s) to the property that is/are the subject of this Assignment:

This Assignment is completed on this _____ day of _____, 201__.

_____   _____
By: For Turnkey Home Buyers   Signature

_____   _____
By: (Print) Assignee   Signature of Assignee

_____   _____
Witness: By: (Print)   Signature of Witness

Wholesaling also involves far less risk. Once I educate you on the intricacies of writing contracts, you will be able to limit and control the amount of risk you incur. I will show you how to write contingencies into your contracts that benefit and protect you. There is nothing underhanded in any of this; it is all completely above board. This is simply what smart investors do.

Part of my job in these educational materials is to teach you all the different ways you can control a property for a certain period of time with very little money down, while insulating yourself from any risk.

Another benefit of wholesaling is how immune assigned contracts are from the macro market trends. Real estate markets fluctuate very little from week to week. By getting in and out of properties quickly, you insulate yourself from potential negative changes in market conditions that can hurt you if you are over exposed at the wrong time. (More about this in Chapter 11, "Learn From My Mistakes.")

A great plus to wholesaling is you don't need perfect credit to wholesale. You often won't need financing. The art of wholesaling is getting in and out quickly. You will be selling your contract to purchase the house. No credit or financing will be necessary

Now that you now know what wholesaling is, let me teach you how it gets done.

You are now up and running in the real estate business. You have your power team in place. You have a developing social media presence, expanding and refining your real estate investor network. You have learned to find properties with upside value in your area, you are able to finance and fix them up, you know how to market them effectively, and with your real estate license, or in conjunction with a realtor, you are able to sell properties. You have it all together. You are in the game now.

As you are noticing, all sorts of entities are buying and selling real estate with a variety of investment strategies. We have spent a great deal of time focusing on identifying properties. There is also great profit potential in identifying investors and being able to provide them what they want in a timely manner. Allow me to explain this last point in greater detail.

Becoming a wholesaler is an easy way to make money in real estate with virtually no financial risk to you. To be successful at this, you need to become an expert matchmaker, a master in the art of knowing what the investors in our network like and finding it for them.

This type of matchmaking happens to all of us every day. Let's take the online world. Our data is being collected by marketers everywhere. They learn our tendencies, what we like and when we like it. A consumer profile of us is being built. It is being updated and refined constantly, without our awareness of the process. Then one day you run a Google search or you take a quick glance at your Facebook timeline, and there they are. Ads. Ads for your favorite clothing, deals on tickets for your favorite band. A click here, another click there, and you are online shopping. Before you know it, you are heading to the checkout line with your cyber cart full of all your favorite stuff.

What just happened there? What happened is the internet marketing consultants did an excellent job compiling a profile of you and all that you like. They succeeded at putting buyer and seller together with a product that enticed. What I am teaching you here in the real estate investing world is really no different. There is profit in finding properties for the investors in your network; putting buyers and sellers together. If we are successful at this, we will be clearing a nice profit for ourselves with every deal.

It's not as hard as you may think. We have all walked onto a car lot. Put ten customers on a huge car lot, throw in a thousand different cars out there, and you will see the art of matchmaking. The question is who is going to buy what, and why? A good car salesman can figure that out in a heartbeat. From the moment you walk on the lot, he's reading the customers. They want to invest in a car. The salesman assesses the buyers, creates a quick profile for them all, and attempts to match them up with the right vehicle on his lot. That's his job, to match buyer to product. The advantage we have in real estate investing is we are going to know our investors much, much better than the salesman on the car lot.

This is an example of the importance of developing precise profiles for the investors in your network. If you have ever been on a car lot looking to buy and the salesman keeps putting you in the wrong vehicle, you are going to grow impatient with him, and likely start looking for someone else to help you with your purchase. It's no different in real estate. The challenge dealing with assigned contracts is the small window of time we control the property. You need to know the profiles of your investors in your network as well as you know yourself. If you keep proposing deals to your investors that are not right for them, not only will you not be making deals, you will be wasting lots of time in the process while risking that your investor clients will find more agreeable deals with other brokers.

There is great profit potential in wholesaling in assignable contracts. You can profit from simply putting properties in the hands of buyers with minimal risk to yourself and a quick turnaround. This is as close to risk-free real estate investing as you can get. And the better you know the investors in your network, the quicker you will start making money in real estate.

Here's how you can develop your investor profiles:

Investor Buying Questionnaire

Buyers Information:

Name: _____	Spouse Name: _____
Address: _____	Address: _____
Home Phone: _____	Home Phone: _____
Mobil Phone: _____	Mobil Phone: _____
Email: _____	Email: _____
Fax: _____	Fax: _____

Funding Information

Funds to purchase investment property will come from:
$ _____ Amount USD   _____ Cash
                                _____ Private Financing   [ ] Have financing
                                                              [ ] Need Financing

Title Information:

Property Title to be taken in the name of. - (Check one)

_____ Individual Name: _____   SS# ___-__-____

_____ LLC / Corp Name: _____   EIN __-_____

Mailing Address:

Address: _____

_____

_____

Property Information:

Type of Property: (Check One)   Type of Service: (Check One)
[ ] Single Family Home   [ ] I am interested in Buy, Fix and Rent
[ ] Condos   [ ] I am interested in Buying only, I will fix and either
[ ] Multi Units/Commercial   keep or sell the property myself

Chapter Eight
How I Mastered Renovating Affordably Along With Creating Maximum Value

If you grew up in the 1990s watching the comedy series "Home Improvement," you've likely shared some laughs at the main character Tim and how spectacularly accident-prone he could be. There seemed no limit to what could go wrong within his renovating projects.

As someone in the real estate investing world, I now cringe at what I used to laugh at. Every accident I see now on a property under repair I see as something cutting into profits. What I want to share with you here is how to assure renovation jobs get done within budget and on time, with as few profit sapping mistakes as possible, so you can experience the same types of success I have.

If you are new to real estate investing, let me be clear. The rehabbing portion of your project requires the most education of all the various aspects a deal entails. We've all heard the horror stories of those who choose to learn on the job. My responsibility to you is to educate you to the best of my abilities as to the intricacies of rehabbing properties. Rehabbing is where you can generate the most profit if you know what you are doing.

The true talent of a real estate investor is to be able to see the potential of a property, to dream the house beautiful. Most times you will find a property below market value because it is not pretty. It needs work. Sometimes it is just a few cosmetic improvements needed, other times it may be major renovations. Your job as an investor is to be able project a vision of the house and property as it could be; both inside and out, and then determine what it would cost to make the vision a reality. If you are not careful, this is where the dream can become a nightmare. You might lose out on a great deal because you overestimated the price of the rehab, or worse, find yourself in a money pit,

The rehabbing portion of the real estate industry has always been my favorite. I was able to work closely with my brother and father for many years on all sorts of renovations. There were so many levels of satisfaction in these projects: helping the seller sell his home; helping the buyer, often a first time home buyer, find a great property to call their own; making good money for my family and me; but most of all, taking great pride in improving the quality of a neighborhood for the locals of a community. There is no better advertising of our skills than positive word of mouth from work done right.

Understand going in, we can't renovate everything. We don't have the time or the resources. We have to make some hard but informed choices as to what our finished product will look like to attract a quick and satisfactory sale price. And we are on a schedule. Time is money, and when it comes to cost and overruns, that's your money. We must be careful about getting caught up in properties that need major renovations. Personally, I tried to choose homes that I could get in and out of within four weeks.

Benjamin Franklin once said, "If you fail to plan, you are planning to fail." Every successful rehab must begin with a plan broken down into several clear, concise stages.

The first step to a successful rehab is a Worksheet checklist that itemizes exactly what your contractors need to address for the renovation. This is fairly straightforward. It is done by listing the areas in the home and on the grounds that need work and what should be done to each. The Worksheet should also list all the materials you want the contractor to use with cost estimates.

An experienced contractor should have a clear vision of the work you want done and how the finished product should look. This is crucial, for contractors will be able to give you far more accurate estimates for the costs of the job. Additionally, a strong Worksheet allows you to formulate a precise payment schedule for work completed. As your business grows and you have multiple properties being rehabbed simultaneously, you will see the importance of being highly organized and detailed in this space. A worksheet is shown at the end of this chapter. How to use it will be discussed in detail at a live workshop or with your coach.

Just prior to beginning your rehab, you will want to do a more thorough walkthrough of the property. Here are a couple ideas of things to bring with you.

A camera. I cannot stress enough the importance of bringing a camera with you, particularly one with a wide lens that can pull in the whole property. A picture really is worth a thousand words. The before and after shots of a renovation will be some of your strongest future marketing tools. Take lots of pictures, from inside the home, as well as numerous angles from the curb.

Signage. Also bring with you some signage for your services. This is free advertising; by all means take advantage of it. You've driven by your share of homes under repair. We all slow down to take a look. Make sure your signs are front and center for those who pass by your renovations.

A lock box. Be sure to place a lock box on the property with keys available for your contractor. It will save you valuable time over the long run not having to wait on others. Remember, time is money in real estate. The more time we are spending on non income generating activities, the less efficient and profitable our business will be.

Choosing a Contractor...

When I was just starting out, as I said, I was fortunate to have my family close by to fulfill my contracting needs. As my business began to expand and my contracting team could not handle all the work themselves, I had to look to my real estate investing network to find qualified help.

What I did when I needed to hire a contractor for a rehab job was to make copies of my Worksheet and leave them at the property. I would invite a number of contractors to the site and ask them to fill out the Worksheet as accurately as possible with their full estimated costs for labor and materials. You will want at minimum three bids from your prospective contractors. If he chooses to subcontract out some work, again, have him provide a minimum of three estimates. Continue to stress the importance of having strong financial controls over your costs. Even if you have a preferred contractor in mind, keep them honest by informing them you are taking bids from other sources. And by all means, reward good work. I made it a staple of my business relationships to pay bonuses to my crews that got the job done either on time or under budget. Don't underestimate the value of a little generosity.

Once you've evaluated all the bids and made your final decision, it's time to sign the contracts and get your rehab project underway. The independent contractor agreement is the heart and soul of your business arrangement. It outlines all the areas crucial to your success; timelines, warranties, insurance, penalties etc. I cannot stress emphatically enough that everyone must sign the documents before any work begins. It's imperative that as an investor you protect yourself. Things can go wrong or go long. It's crucial that your hired contractor be held accountable to the work he has agreed to do by signing his name to your work contract. Also know that if permits are required, most municipalities require that the contractor is licensed and insured.

Other documents of importance here are Insurance Indemnification forms the contractor needs to have; W9 tax forms in order to 1099 all your contractors for their tax liability; Final and Unconditional Waiver of Lien forms to protect you against any fraudulent claims against your property; and most importantly a payment schedule, which specifically lays out the agreed upon timeline for payments between you and your contractor.

Let me stress. Don't be intimidated by all the requirements that go into a deal. Most all of what I am suggesting here is actually quite simple when dealt with individually. This is simply what smart investors do. They protect themselves at every turn against risk and possible overruns within the project. What this paperwork does is it holds everybody on your team accountable for their part.

Once work commences, depending upon how busy you are and your managerial style, you will want to develop a good working relationship with your contractor. This is a win-win situation if handled well with repeat business down the road a near certainty. I personally was not one to look over the shoulder of my contractor micromanaging his every move. That said, I did make it a point to stop by the work site every day to check in to make sure repairs were being done in an orderly and timely fashion. Nobody works well being over-scrutinized, yet to not monitor the renovation progress would be irresponsible business. The quicker we get our projects to market, the quicker we get paid. My best advice here is to find a professional balance with those you contract to work for you that works best for all parties.

Curb appeal. We can spend all this time and energy repairing and renovating, but if we neglect to landscape the property, prospective buyers will never stop their cars. We must make it a priority to have our properties look inviting. We can't showcase the renovations of our power team if they never make it to the front door. It's our responsibility as real estate investors to maximize curb appeal. Our homes have to look good. Our clients have to be able to see themselves pulling up to that property every day and be proud to call it home.

Finally, stay organized. There are many important documents that need to be signed and filed for easy access. Stay on top of the details. As your business grows and you have several rehabs going at once, having your office in a tight orderly fashion will make your workdays run far more smoothly.

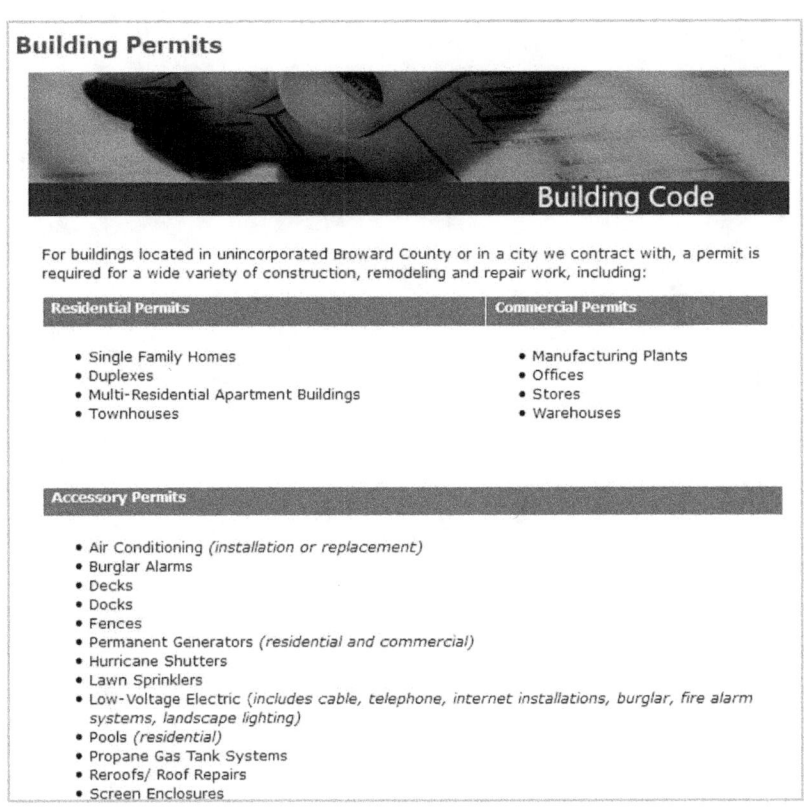

Building Permits

Building Code

For buildings located in unincorporated Broward County or in a city we contract with, a permit is required for a wide variety of construction, remodeling and repair work, including:

Residential Permits	Commercial Permits
• Single Family Homes • Duplexes • Multi-Residential Apartment Buildings • Townhouses	• Manufacturing Plants • Offices • Stores • Warehouses

Accessory Permits

- Air Conditioning *(installation or replacement)*
- Burglar Alarms
- Decks
- Docks
- Fences
- Permanent Generators *(residential and commercial)*
- Hurricane Shutters
- Lawn Sprinklers
- Low-Voltage Electric *(includes cable, telephone, internet installations, burglar, fire alarm systems, landscape lighting)*
- Pools *(residential)*
- Propane Gas Tank Systems
- Reroofs/ Roof Repairs
- Screen Enclosures

And do not cut corners. If major renovations are being done, permits need to be pulled with city officials and local building departments. It is really important to have good relationships with these bureaucracies. There will come a day when you need something from them much quicker than they may feel like providing it. Your relationship with them will determine with what speed your needs are met. Treat these people well regardless; your team is your future. They are like silent partners to your hoped for success and great people to have on your side.

Every rehab will be different. There are small quick repairs and major renovations. Obviously I am giving you here a general overview of the process. There is still much more to learn within the details of your rehabs. My point in this chapter is to show you through being organized, diligent, and professional, you will be forging quality business relationships throughout your local real estate community that will lead to the kind of long-term financial success I have been fortunate to achieve.

Renovation Punch-Out Checklist
"Things To Look For"

1.	All plate and switch covers - all must be on.	Good	Poor	Not at All
2.	All plugs and switches - no open wires.	Good	Poor	Not at All
3.	All lights and fans installed - no loose wires hanging out anywhere.	Good	Poor	Not at All
4.	Turn on all sinks and flush all toilets and look for any leaks or problems flushing.	Good	Poor	Not at All
5.	Check all windows and make sure they open, close, and lock properly - no broken glass, no missing screens or ripped screens.	Good	Poor	Not at All
6.	Check all door knobs to see that they lock properly and are all installed.	Good	Poor	Not at All
7.	Open and shut all doors and make sure they work properly - all should go over carpet smoothly, no missing doors and no holes in doors or grayed bottoms.	Good	Poor	Not at All
8.	Exterior doors - check to see that they all have thresholds and no room at bottom for bugs to get in. Hint if you see daylight coming in, it needs attention.	Good	Poor	Not at All
9.	Check all kitchen cabinets and bath vanity doors - all should close and stay closed and all should have handles.	Good	Poor	Not at All
10.	All appliances should work properly and have knobs in place.	Good	Poor	Not at All
11.	Showers and tubs should work properly - shower cut on should work as well as drains, no loose or missing tiles, no uncaulked holes around handles and no cracks for water to seep through.	Good	Poor	Not at All
12.	All areas where there is water for example, kitchen, bath and laundry - the plugs should be FGI's which means there is a little "test" and "reset" button on it.	Good	Poor	Not at All
13.	AC and heat should work properly - check both by turning on and placing hand near a vent.	Good	Poor	Not at All
14.	All closet doors if bifolds ar sliders should be smooth and stay on track.	Good	Poor	Not at All
15.	There should be no missing baseboards.	Good	Poor	Not at All
16.	Carpet and vinyl should be laid completely and no curling up of vinyl.	Good	Poor	Not at All
17.	NO evidence of water stains on the ceiling or walls.	Good	Poor	Not at All
18.	Interior and exterior fully painted 100%.	Good	Poor	Not at All
19.	Exterior paint - no noticeable cracking or peeling of paint.	Good	Poor	Not at All
20.	No evidence of any rotted wood on soffit or fascia or body of the house.	Good	Poor	Not at All
21.	No ripped or unattached screens on porches as applicable.	Good	Poor	Not at All
22.	All caulking complete as needed - just noticeable areas such as baths and kitchens and base boards.	Good	Poor	Not at All
23.	No rust spots or worn areas in sinks.	Good	Poor	Not at All
24.	No nicks in the tubs surface.	Good	Poor	Not at All

25. No large noticeable cracks or areas where laminate is broken on countertops. Good   Poor   Not at All
26. Grass cut - just not unrealistically high. Past the ankles gets bad. Good   Poor   Not at All
27. All debris and trash inside and outside of the house removed. Good   Poor   Not at All
28. All doors that may hit the wall should have door stops. Good   Poor   Not at All
19. No holes in the drywall. Good   Poor   Not at All
30. No missing exterior lights and globes. All lights should have protective globes. Good   Poor   Not at All
31. All ceiling fans work and no missing lights or wires hanging loose. Good   Poor   Not at All
32. Hot water checked by turning on. Good   Poor   Not at All
33. No roof leaks or missing shingles if visible - good to have a ladder. Good   Poor   Not at All
34. Mirrors, medicine cabinets, towel bars and toilet paper holders all intact. Good   Poor   Not at All
35. No missing doorbells - again no loose wires. Good   Poor   Not at All
36. Washer and dryer water lines intact and water heater hooked up and dryer plug intact - you should never see loose wires unprotected. Good   Poor   Not at All
37. Look at all exterior door frames and look for rotted wood on trim. Good   Poor   Not at All
38. All closets should have shelves and clothes rods, at least a place to hang clothes. Good   Poor   Not at All
39. All ac holes must be covered with vents, no open holes. Good   Poor   Not at All
40. Check all light switches and plugs - I have a tester for the plugs. Good   Poor   Not at All
41. All exterior water spigots should have no leaks, should have handles and should work properly. Good   Poor   Not at All
42. Breaker boxes should have a cover door. Good   Poor   Not at All
43. Ceiling attic access holes should have covers, not open. Good   Poor   Not at All
44. AC doors must always be vented. Good   Poor   Not at All
45. Garbage disposal, if there is one must work properly. Good   Poor   Not at All
46. All homes must have readable house numbers and a mailbox. Good   Poor   Not at All
47. Pools should be checked by professionals. Good   Poor   Not at All

Property Address: _____
Owner Name: _____
Contractor's Name: _____
Contractor's Phone: _____

Exhibit "D"

TURNKEY HOME BUYERS

Item	Description	Needed Quantities	Item Cost Per	Contractor #1	Draw #1	Draw #2	Draw #3
Exterior							
Roof				$ -	$ -	$ -	$ -
Gutters				$ -	$ -	$ -	$ -
Foundation				$ -	$ -	$ -	$ -
Grading				$ -	$ -	$ -	$ -
Siding				$ -	$ -	$ -	$ -
Paint	Outside paint job			$ -	$ -	$ -	$ -
Carpentry				$ -	$ -	$ -	$ -
Soffit / Fascia / Trim				$ -	$ -	$ -	$ -
Windows / Screens	Replace - instalation included			$ -	$ -	$ -	$ -
Windows / Screens	Repair - instalation included			$ -	$ -	$ -	$ -
Doors				$ -	$ -	$ -	$ -
Deck / Porch				$ -	$ -	$ -	$ -
Screening	Repair/place			$ -	$ -	$ -	$ -
Garage Door				$ -	$ -	$ -	$ -
Driveway	Resurfacing			$ -	$ -	$ -	$ -
Fence				$ -	$ -	$ -	$ -
Landscaping/Curb Appeal	New Sod front and back/			$ -		$ -	$ -
Plants	New throughout			$ -	$ -	$ -	$ -
Termite Treatment				$ -	$ -	$ -	$ -
Walkway				$ -	$ -	$ -	$ -
Other				$ -	$ -	$ -	$ -
Other				$ -	$ -	$ -	$ -
Other				$ -	$ -	$ -	$ -
Mechanical / Systems							
Heater				$ -	$ -	$ -	$ -
HVAC Ducts	Service			$ -		$ -	$ -
Air-Conditioner	2.5 ton =< 1500 sq ft [used $1,000]			$ -	$ -	$ -	$ -
Electrical - Rough	200 Amp			$ -	$ -	$ -	$ -
Light Fixtures				$ -	$ -	$ -	$ -
Plumbing - Rough				$ -	$ -	$ -	$ -
Hot Water Heater				$ -	$ -	$ -	$ -
Plumming HWH				$ -	$ -	$ -	$ -
Clean Drains				$ -	$ -	$ -	$ -
Sewer Hook up				$ -	$ -	$ -	$ -
Septic Tank Abandment				$ -	$ -	$ -	$ -
AC Sevicing				$ -	$ -	$ -	$ -
Other				$ -	$ -	$ -	$ -
Other				$ -	$ -	$ -	$ -
Interior Finish							
Walls / Ceilings / Trim	Drywall & labor			$ -	$ -	$ -	$ -
Wall Plates & Switches				$ -	$ -	$ -	$ -
Ceiling Fans	Includes Labor			$ -		$ -	$ -
Front Door				$ -	$ -	$ -	$ -
Regular Doors + Hardware	New doors throughout			$ -		$ -	$ -
Paint	inside paint throughout			$ -		$ -	$ -
Flooring	New carpet throughout			$ -		$ -	$ -
Acid Wash Tile				$ -	$ -	$ -	$ -
Other				$ -	$ -	$ -	$ -
Other				$ -	$ -	$ -	$ -
Other				$ -	$ -	$ -	$ -
Other				$ -	$ -	$ -	$ -

Kitchen									
Cabinets	New kitchen cabinets		$	-	$	-	$	-	$	-
Countertop	New		$	-			$	-	$	-
Sink	New		$	-	$	-	$	-	$	-
Faucet			$	-	$	-	$	-	$	-
Flooring	Kitchen and Laundry Room		$	-			$	-	$	-
Appliances			$	-	$	-	$	-	$	-
Referigerator			$	-	$	-	$	-	$	-
Stove			$	-	$	-	$	-	$	-
Dish Washer			$	-	$	-	$	-	$	-
Install Dishwasher			$	-	$	-	$	-	$	-
Other			$	-	$	-	$	-	$	-
Other			$	-	$	-	$	-	$	-
Other			$	-	$	-	$	-	$	-
Master Bathroom									
Vanity	New		$	-	$	-	$	-	$	-
Sink	New		$	-	$	-	$	-	$	-
Shower Head & Harware			$	-	$	-	$	-	$	-
Tub	Replace		$	-	$	-	$	-	$	-
Shower / Surround		0	$	-	$	-	$	-	$	-
Toilet	New		$	-	$	-	$	-	$	-
Bathroom Flooring/Tile			$	-	$	-	$	-	$	-
Glass Shower Door			$	-	$	-	$	-	$	-
Plumming			$	-	$	-	$	-	$	-
Other			$	-	$	-	$	-	$	-
Other			$	-	$	-	$	-	$	-
Other			$	-	$	-	$	-	$	-
Other Bathroom									
Vanity	New		$	-	$	-	$	-	$	-
Sink	New		$	-	$	-	$	-	$	-
Shower Head & Harware			$	-	$	-	$	-	$	-
Tub	Replace		$	-	$	-	$	-	$	-
Shower / Surround	Spray Brand New		$	-	$	-	$	-	$	-
Toilet			$	-	$	-	$	-	$	-
Bathroom Flooring/Tile	NEW		$	-	$	-	$	-	$	-
Glass Shower Dorr			$	-	$	-	$	-	$	-
Plumming			$	-	$	-	$	-	$	-
Mirror & medicine cabinet			$	-	$	-	$	-	$	-
Other			$	-	$	-	$	-	$	-
Other			$	-	$	-	$	-	$	-
Other			$	-	$	-	$	-	$	-
Other			$	-	$	-	$	-	$	-
Other			$	-	$	-	$	-	$	-
Other			$	-	$	-	$	-	$	-
Miscellaneous									
Demo / Cleanout			$	-			$	-	$	-
Final Cleaning	Maid Service		$	-			$	-	$	-
Dumpsters			$	-	$	-	$	-	$	-
Permits			$	-	$	-	$	-	$	-
Permits			$	-	$	-	$	-	$	-
Permits			$	-	$	-	$	-	$	-
Admin			$	-			$	-	$	-
Other			$	-			$	-	$	-
Other			$	-			$	-	$	-
Other			$	-	$	-	$	-	$	-
TOTAL			$	-	$	-	$	-	$	-

Chapter Nine
Renting And Selling Strategies That Turn Profits Into Reality

The housing market. We've all lived through a few cycles: the booms, the busts. One moment a new development is built and dozens of homes are sold within hours. Other times, interest rates soar, prices plunge, credit tightens and foreclosures are everywhere. It can all sound a bit overwhelming at times. How do we as real estate investors know whether to be in the market or not?

I would not be sharing my experiences in the real estate industry with you if I did not feel now was an excellent time to be in the market. As I write this, I am personally actively investing in the market. It's been my experience that smart real estate investors always find good deals in any marketplace regardless. What I want to share with you now are the basic standards to selling or renting your newly rehabbed properties that will always be applicable regardless of whether overall market conditions are hot or not.

If you apply the educational materials here in this book as well as from my seminars, you will soon have property in rehab coming close to completion. The light at the end of the tunnel is your profit rapidly approaching. All the research, due diligence, attention to detail, and hard work are coming to fruition. But don't celebrate too fast. We still have a completed property to rent or sell. What is the most effective way to achieve these final steps?

There are so many variables involved in how best to exit your property. Where you live, the neighborhood of your property, the price of your property. The renting process is relatively simple. While you can manage your own rental property, it is a good idea to use a management company. Below are the services that a good management company would provide, or things that you would need to perform. An internet search will provide several leads for management companies. As with the contractor, you will need to interview several to find the one that is right for you.

Advertise your rental

Handle tenant inquiries

Background and credit investigations

Application processing

Lease signing

Full service repair

Rent collection

Accounting

Handle Tenant complaints

Coordinate Evictions

Marketing Makes the Difference

Rental property doesn't lease itself. Every day that your home sits vacant costs you money. It doesn't take but a month or two before you're in a cash-negative position.

Setting the right price is key. You need to know the neighborhood and what the market will bear.

You will need to do a thorough application process, including extensive credit and background checks.

If a renter doesn't maintain your property, you could see its value plunge. You will need to let the tenants know that you are hands-on property managers. They can easily contact you if a maintenance situation arises.

For one of my properties in Orlando I found an incredible property management company. Here is the marketing approach that they sent to me:

With the real estate market changing so much in the last few years, it is more important than ever to have as much advertising placed as possible. Our advertising consists of:

1. 100 plus websites (www.realtor.com, www.zillow.com, www.trulia.com, www.craigslist.com, etc.)
2. A Multiple Listing Service (MLS) AD. We pay the referral to other agents.
3. NEW TECHNOLOGY, 10 Mobile Applications for IOS and Android Devices.
4. Signs if allowed per the HOA.
5. We will also use Facebook, Twitter, Linked-In, and Blog about your property to encourage more calls.
6. There's more! We duplicate all of our listings into Spanish and update daily, www.alquileresymanejodepropiedades.com, and then place www.Craiglist.com ads directing Spanish speaking tenants to our Spanish website.
7. Plus we answer calls 7 days a week, show properties 7 days a week.

Basically we will stop at nothing to let potential tenants know about your property. **MORE ADS = MORE CALLS = MORE SHOWINGS = A GREAT TENANT!**

Our property rented in just 5 days with them If your team is not doing all of these things, you will have the success I have had with my rental properties.

At the seminars or through your coaching sessions, we will walk you through the rental process and how to find a management company to add to your power team.

Our alternate exit strategy option besides renting is to sell our properties. If we wholesale a property, our parameters for selling are different than if we rehab. Wholesale selling involves selling the property to other investors and takes place in a much smaller window of time. My focus here is on selling our newly renovated homes at full market value to qualified homeowners.

The timing of when you put the "For Sale" sign up is critical to your profitability. You cannot put your house on the market before it is repaired. That said, you do not have to wait until all work is complete. A general rule I apply is putting the home on the market two weeks before the rehab is complete. With two weeks to go, the property should look appealing to a prospective buyer. This gives you a little extra time to find a buyer and should cut down on your holding costs.

Here is a list of some of the important aspects of selling your property. This is by no means complete, but more a general overview of the task at hand.

Hiring an Agent. I recommend that in time that you become a licensed realtor yourself. Prior to doing so, you will not likely have a lengthy buyers list developed. For this reason I recommend you go with an experienced real estate agent from your area. Sure, it cuts into profits some, but a strong selling agent over the long haul will be more than worth whatever commissions must be paid out.

If there is any one industry that is more misunderstood than a realtor I would like to see it. The perception is that a couple of signs get put up, an ad gets placed in the paper here or there, and buyers flock to the property, ready to sign their names on the dotted line. That's just not the truth. Selling properties, especially in distressed markets during tight credit times, is complex. We do not have the luxury to learn this skill on the job; every month your house sits idle is another month of financing charges cutting in to your profits.

A good agent will handle marketing the home, meeting with potential buyers, and will take care of the many aspects of the closing process. A standard fee for a realtor is in the five to six percent range. A good one is worth every bit of that. For your investment to turn to profit the property must sell, so do not take any unnecessary chances in this area.

Agreements. There are options as to what kind of listing agreements you can sign with a realtor. Most realtors will want to sign Exclusive Right-to-Sell agreements. It gives the individual realtor the right to earn a commission if the property sells during the time he or she lists it. Logically you might think that having multiple realtors contracted to sell your property would be advantageous to you. In reality, a realtor is not going to give your property the same priority if there is a chance the selling commission will not come to them. Having an experienced reputable realtor with an exclusive agreement is the best way to assure their maximum focus at getting your house sold at the best possible price for all parties.

Going Solo. In time, you may build a sizable buyers list and decide to start marketing and selling your renovated houses on your own without a realtor. Here are some of what I believe to be the best strategies for this.

Signage. The most popular sign in America is still "For Sale By Owner." Signs are a close second to the internet in generating leads for prospective buyers. A catchy sign can leave a lasting imprint in the minds of buyers and sellers alike. Get your signage up early and often on your properties and draw the prospective buyers to you.

Websites. There are popular property listing websites like Craigslist, Zillow, and Trulia as well as many more. Recent studies have shown that 80% of buyers now start their home searches on the internet. It's crucial to have a high visibility presence on as many of these sites as possible, depending on the number of listings you have.

Social Media. It is mandatory that we utilize our ever-growing social media networks to list our renovated homes. Picture-friendly sites like Facebook and Instagram are great resources for showcasing our rehabs before and after work. A strong presence here is part of our pathway to real estate investing success.

Neighborhood. Think locally. Tactfully spread the word to neighbors of your property that your rehab will be coming on the market as a rental or sale. People love to have family members or close friends living close by. Word of mouth from those in the neighborhood can be the easiest way to close out your property. A smart letter to those in the community can make your hoped for sale fall in to place quite quickly.

There are lots of other particulars to get into here when screening home buyers....credit checks, building inspections etc. As you continue to build your power team and expand your networks, you will be doing business with highly qualified and competent agents in all these respective fields. You are building mutually beneficial business relationships with all these parties. Remember, continue to make yourself attractive and you will attract the best of the best your real estate community has to offer.

This is it. This is how it gets done. From identifying a potential property to that final signature to close the deal. There's a lot to this, but all of it is highly achievable. I was a kid who came from nothing who knew little to nothing about real estate. But I was willing to learn. My success has come strictly from my desire to live a life of wealth and abundance, the exact same traits that you possess that have you reading my book here wanting the same things I have been so fortunate to achieve.

Everything I've described to you here has been happening in every neighborhood in America for decades and will continue on into the future indefinitely. The time is now for you to get your piece of the pie as you pursue your financial dreams in real estate investing. Though I've had great success, I've also slipped a few times along the way. In the next couple of chapters I plan to tell you about some of my ups and downs in the hopes you can learn from both.

Chapter Ten
How To Turn Your Network Into Your Future Net Worth

It's hard to remember back to how the world once was before the explosion of social media and smart phones. We are all connected to each other constantly in ways once thought unimaginable. As aspiring real estate investors, it's important that we navigate this changing landscape as wisely as possible.

As individuals, to not participate in social media is a personal choice. Some people prefer to keep their private lives private. But if our goal is financial abundance, our net worth will only be as good as our network. Social media is a great medium to broaden our exposure.

We would all like to be able to sit back with our laptops, make eye-catching targeted posts to the parties within our real estate investor network, and watch the business roll in. That is what I would refer to as a passive contact, interacting with someone we have yet to meet in person or in direct conversation. It's not impossible to generate business in this way, but it's unlikely the best way to assure ourselves of our desired life of wealth and abundance.

My best advice for you is to take your newly formed social media connections and make them real life connections as quickly as possible. We would never do important business with someone we've never met or spoken with. That will cut both ways. If your network connections are hesitant to communicate in person with you, do not waste time here. We are serious about our work. Choose only to deal with similarly driven people.

Social media is a great way to put yourself in all the right circles for aspiring investors. But more so, it plays an equally important role in advertising and marketing your power team and your brand. I encourage you to take your power team viral. Tell everyone about your team, about the projects you're working on. Talk about your successes in a respectful professional way. Show the industry who you are and that you are open for business.

Here are some pointers for you to give you an advantage when engaging this ever-changing field.

Be responsible. A lot of this is common sense, but you would be stunned if you saw how many ambitious entrepreneurs make the mistake of mixing their personal life with their professional business. If we've all learned anything over the past five years of social media expansion, people don't really want to read about your politics. Once people are within your network, they have already approved of you. Their role in your life is as a potential business partner, not as a running mate for political office. We are a nation divided. Keep your politics to yourself. By expressing yourself in that way, you are essentially disqualifying yourself from half your possible connections. The idea here is to grow our networks, not alienate them.

Also realize that social media is a permanent record. Assume everything you post online is going to be seen by the most influential people in all of real estate. Whether it is through your personal or professional social media outlets, think before you post. Notice how many people have had their careers or personal lives severely impacted because of a Facebook post or a tweet. There have been celebrities, politicians and ordinary people who have had to scramble to try and undo damage done by a casual post that was not well planned. Once it is out there, it is out there.

Image and tone. Pay close attention to what works for you and what does not. What you like, others will like. Be positive, be upbeat, and be inspirational. Share yourself, share your story, your dreams, and your ambitions. Think about it. You do not socialize with people you don't care for. Social media is no different. People are going to come across your name and image frequently throughout the day. It's imperative to impart an image of class and professionalism.

Catch their eye. Do not be generic. Find a style or something unique about you that best represents you. You do not have to be a web genius to be successful at this. Imitation is the highest form of flattery. See ideas that work for you and build on them with your own personal accent. People in your network are going to see your posts often but only for a moment. Be sure to be attractive to their scrolling eyes.

Be patient. It may appear that others are way ahead of you in social media. Remember, five years ago the field barely existed. Everyone is learning as they go. There have been growing pains for everyone in this area. Facebook, Twitter, Instagram and LinkedIn are the major players in this area. You will want a presence on all of these. In time, something new will come along to challenge them. I believe strongly in staying abreast of developments in this area. Having someone on your power team who has Internet savvy is a huge plus, but is not mandatory. Most of this can be learned if you commit some time to it daily.

Be efficient. We all spend too much idle time in the social media world. It's ultimately harmless, but if making a name for ourselves as real estate investors is our goal, there are better uses of our time. The primary usefulness of social media is for exposure. Everyone in your network is going to see your posts, so don't get caught up in the analytics. If you have a website and make a blog post, some of the websites provide tremendous amount of information as to who is looking at your site. A little bit of analysis here is fine, but use your time wisely. If they are serious about doing business, they will contact you, just as you make contact with the firms and entrepreneurs you want to learn more about.

Free advertising. A major aspect of social media is free advertising. If you paid for a billboard sign in your community, you wouldn't waste your time parked underneath your sign counting how many cars drove by. Don't do this with social media either. People are seeing your posts. Folks spend far more time on social media than they care to admit. Its natural when you have a blog, website, or social media accounts to pay close attention to your numbers; page views, likes, retweets and the sort. Web statistics can be misleading. You are looking for people to invest in real estate with you, not get likes and retweets. Serious people have real relationships. Get on the phone, email, attend meet-and-greets. People aren't doing these events for their health. They want to expand their businesses just like you.

Take charge. Don't wait for your contacts to approach you. Take control of your connections. Reach out. Respond back. Send private messages saying welcome or thank you. Acknowledge milestones in their lives, birthdays, anniversaries, be a positive supportive connection, a unifier, not a divider. If your situation permits, organize local get-togethers. An online network must be converted in to real life business contacts otherwise they lack any meaningful value.
Social media will open so many more doors for you; it's still the job of your power team to close the door on the deals you make.

Build your network. I have a database of 23,000 names of people who have attended my seminars over the years, well before the explosion of social media. I built my network the old fashioned way — I met them all. It took time, but they all are there, and many are still there I might add. Build your network for the long haul. Not everyone will be an immediate partner for you in your real estate ventures. Be patient. Continue to build your investor profiles so when opportunities do arise in time, you will know immediately where to turn to keep building your business.

Have a strategy. Right from the start I adopted the golden rule to all of my web interactions --treat others like you would like to be treated yourself. Simple, but somehow not easy, as you have seen for yourselves how often people can fail at being pleasant.

Be diligent. Put yourself in positions for good things to happen for your team. If you want the best properties, you have to let everyone and anyone know you are looking to buy (agents, friends, family, networks.)

Don't judge. Famed marketing expert Jim Rohn says "Don't judge. You never know who has what." I could not agree more. Some of my best business transactions came from the most unlikely of sources. It takes practice, but refrain from judging. The person you least suspect may turn out to be your biggest deal.

Chapter Eleven
Learn From My Mistakes

MY THREE BIGGEST MISTAKES.

Sometimes our dreams do not always end the way we thought they would or the way we wanted them to end. But, the successful dreamer knows how to learn the lessons from dreams turned sour. We do not stop dreaming if we have a nightmare, we simply learn how to alter the ending by learning from our mistakes.

Mistake Number One: I did not protect myself.

The term "stress test" received a lot of air time after the recent banking collapse. The term referred to risk management in a worst-case economic scenario for our rebuilding banks. If economic conditions changed drastically over a short period of time, (like they did in 2007-2008), did the banks have enough capital in reserves to ride out the hard times? The stress test applied to the banks to see which ones would remain solvent and which ones would struggle to remain afloat. As real estate investors, we can apply the same type of stress tests to ourselves. As my business expanded throughout the 1990s I wish I had.

My number one mistake in my real estate business was not managing my risk exposure during changing economic times. My deals were structured to get in and get out quickly, with the out portion of the deal dependent on my team's ability to sell our rehabbed property in a timely fashion. At my peak in 1999 I had approximately 80 properties going simultaneously. Everything could not have been going better. But I soon found out I was not ready for the changes that soon came.

My deals were still structured with a hard moneylender who expected a monthly interest payment from my investment partner. Getting in and out of my deals within six months had not been a problem before. But conditions soon turned. With the economy in free fall in late 1999, my properties weren't selling as quickly. That meant little to my hard money lender, who still expected to get his monthly interest payment. As my properties remained vacant, we needed to continue to pay on our fist mortgages. Unfortunately my investment partners at the time were not prepared to ride out the downturn, leaving me to continue to make the payments on the 80 properties or risk losing everything.

The mistake I made was not structuring my deals in ways that assured my investment partners were in for the long haul. You must make sure your investment partners are committed to your rehabs through all the possible ups and downs of the market. By not structuring my deals in ways that insulated me from all the risk of my properties, I made it so my investment partners could walk away with minimal losses, leaving me on the hook for the first mortgages and all that entails.

You must structure your deals such that when conditions turn, your investment partners are committed to continue to write checks to the hard money lenders financing your rehabs. Markets can turn, and turn suddenly. The falloffs can be frightening to those with financial exposure. In reality, down cycles do not last that long. As circumstances played out in my case, I had to liquidate my 80 properties at a substantial discount or face financial ruin. My investor team did not hang in there for the duration of the down cycle, but by 2001 all 80 of those properties were selling in the $120-140k range, with not a one of them with a first mortgage of over 70k. That's an awful lot of money we missed out on strictly from not having my deals structured properly. Make sure you do not make the same mistakes. Find investment partners who will be committed for the long haul.

Mistake Number Two: Losing the TLC in the rehab process.

Part of my enjoyment in rehabbing properties was the pride I could take at improving properties for first time homeowners. My team and I could take properties and make them shine; the before and after pictures were pretty telling. As my business continued to grow, that priority began to diminish. That became a mistake for my business.

Part of rehabbing is having a great product to put on the marketplace. As my business grew rapidly, I began to have to contract out to other less proven contractors to do my renovation work. Additionally, I was purchasing properties for a little more than normal, willing to sell them for a little less than normal. To still pull a profit, less attention was being put in to the rehabbing part of the deals. As market conditions turned, my properties no longer stood out from the pack of other rehabbers. My growth was too quick; my renovations began to not receive the same TLC as before as all aspects of my business began to suffer.

The lesson learned here is stay within your limits. Growing too fast is not a good problem to have. As I grew, I lost control of my power team who, in time, were off making their own investment deals. In retrospect, I wish I had stuck with my original plan of having my team put the most TLC possible into our properties. Instead of expanding up to 80 properties, I would have been just fine working with half of that yet giving each of those properties the TLC they deserved.

Mistake Number Three: not having a short-term, long-term strategy.

The only thing better than splitting a profit check with your investors is splitting lots of profit checks with your investors. During the 1990s my business was hot with all sorts of people wanting to work with my team to make some real estate money. In retrospect, I wish I had not been so quick to turn every property rehabbed into a quick turnaround profit center. If I had kept maybe one out of four, one out of five, and rented them out, today I would own a ton of properties free and clear, collecting monthly rents while watching the properties appreciate in value.

There's a difference between profit and wealth. Keep your eyes open to your larger investment plans. Owning properties free and clear are great ways to diversify your real estate investment business. Keep your eyes open to the properties that may be advantageous to hold onto over the long haul.

Chapter Twelve
Victories That Mean More To Me Than Any Profit I Earned

Anyone who has spent their career in a volatile industry like real estate investing has had their share of ups and downs, moments they are proud of, and experiences they have learned from.

Now that I have shared with you my mistakes, let me tell you about my three greatest personal successes.

1) Developing a rent-to-own program.

The famed philosopher Henry David Thoreau once said, "There is no more noble activity than to positively affect the quality of another person's day."

Something I am very proud of in my career was developing an affordable rent-to-own program in greater Orlando starting with virtually no resources. Looking back on many of my earlier projects, I started to see the work I was engaged in was much more than just something from which to pull a paycheck. What I was really doing was providing an opportunity for financially challenged tenants to share in the American Dream of home ownership. It was great to make a nice profit from my deals. But to materially affect the quality of so many people's lives by helping them get into one of my fixed up houses with a reasonable mortgage, it's something to this day fills me with pride and consider one of my greatest business successes. I think back on how many properties we bought and sold. That's a lot of families we were able to have positively impacted. And to make a great living from it all made it even better.

Whether you feel inspired by these words to go on and do similar rewarding work, or innovate on your own in this amazingly diverse industry by finding your own creative ways to buy and sell real estate, if you are a "people person" like me, you will be moved by how many lives you will affect. There are very few businesses where you get to be a part of the most important purchase a family will make, as well as employing numerous people along the way. The gratification I got when closing a solid deal proved to me this was the industry for me. And to get paid handsomely for it too; I really can't think of a better way to make a living.

2) Becoming a national spokesperson for *Success Magazine*.

Honestly, I was just working hard at my job, trying to stay on top of all my responsibilities. My business was expanding and people outside of my power team were beginning to take notice. *Success Magazine* soon approached me to become involved in some of their infomercial and regional seminar work. Little did I know that public speaking on the subjects outlined here in my book would come so naturally to me. A few years of seminars allowed me to hone my delivery to the thousands of attendees who came to hear me speak. Then I got the notification. My work with *Success Magazine* was being recognized, as I was given an award as one of the top up- and-coming entrepreneurs in the nation. All within six years of my first transaction.

What an honor, to have my ideas and efforts recognized by such a prestigious, national company. I reflect back on it now, wondering how it all fell into place so fast. All I did then is what I am doing with you here now, sharing with you my secrets of success in the real estate investing world. This has always been my passion. Between the seminars and infomercials I was able to reach hundreds of thousands of prospective real estate investors, all from developing and sharing the model laid out for you here in these pages about how to build a real estate business with minimal working capital. Pretty cool stuff. All this despite starting with virtually no working capital; from building strong working relationships, finding those partners that mattered, and executing our plans.

3) How to be a successful real estate investor starting with only a dream.

When I reflect back on all the life projects I've had, whether I was helping young people become great tennis players, helping first-time homeowners buy their first properties, or my work here with you helping you start your own real estate investing business, it sometimes can feel like three entirely different lives. But as I look closer, there are strong consistent threads through all my endeavors.

Through it all I have found that I am a coach at heart. I learned early in life, from some of my earliest tennis experiences, that for any situation to work there must be passion, guidance and leadership. Through a combination of having a strong encouraging mother and a couple of the best coaches a young athlete could ever have, I was able to learn what traits of leadership were effective and what traits were not.

Without the passion and interest shown me I never would have made it as a tennis player, a coach or a business owner. But through my mentors, I learned how to be the best leader, coach and guide I could be.

If I had to sit here and chronicle my number one life success to you it would be how successful so many of the individuals who learned from me became themselves.

The young tennis players I taught and coached who all went on to very successful careers themselves, my first power team I put together who learned the real estate investing business from working with me, where so many of them went on to wildly successful financial careers, to this moment now, where I am writing this book to give to you in the hopes you will learn from my work and strike out on your own path of wealth and abundance.

The greatest reward for me is that those to whom I have taught the ropes have gone on to become great coaches and teachers themselves. When they thank me, not for what I taught them, but for how to teach, that to me is my number one success. They picked up on the best parts of me, the parts that motivate and inspire, the parts that encourage discipline and sacrifice and determination for one's goals. It's these human qualities that will never go out of style and that I strongly believe are the cornerstones of my success and the success of those who have learned from me over the years.

And the type of success I want for you.

*As a young boy I wanted to live the American Dream.
My mother taught me happiness, health and
helping others should be my life's goals. I trusted her
amazing advice and have thrived ever since. This next chapter
represents the qualities I believe it takes to reach your true
God given potential.*

Chapter Thirteen
What Being A "Great American" Means To Me, Will You Join Me?

I like to close my live events and personal appearances by describing what my idea of being a great American is all about. Our nation has an illustrious history of innovators and entrepreneurs who had the courage to lay it all on the line. All the great visionaries and dreamers of our past had the courage to follow their dreams because we live in a society that rewards those who dream big and aren't afraid to go after a life of wealth and abundance, and lay it all on the line as they go for it.

Here's how I break down what it means to be a great American.

A IS FOR...ATTITUDE. The great Americans that have inspired me all have great attitudes: positive, upbeat, always seeing the good in everybody and everything. They all lead by example, and they always plan for a better future in spite of any hardships they endured. They know how to ride out tough times. They never burn bridges. They plant seeds for success to harvest some future day. They inspire and motivate all who come in contact with them. I have done everything in my power to practice these types of principles in all my life's affairs.

M IS FOR...MISSION. Your dreams and vision become your mission. It's about an unwavering determination to be successful; a laser sharp focus on the goal at hand. A no excuses manner of going after what one desires. Nobody can stop someone on a mission. For me, whether it was becoming the best tennis player I could be or becoming a successful real estate investor, I wasn't going to allow anything to get in my way. Define your mission and do not be denied.

E IS FOR...EDUCATION. Knowledge is power. Who do we learn from? We learn the most from the people who know more than us. Surround yourself with the most knowledgeable people you can. Read the brightest and smartest in our industry. We will never know it all. Speak less, listen more. I learn little when I'm doing all the talking. As someone without a college education, I made little pretense that I was the smartest guy in the room. But I made it part of my mission to learn everything I could from those who were. Make it part of yours.

R IS FOR...RELIGION. For me, religion is the foundation of my inspiration. I can hardly imagine a world without some higher purpose. Personally, I am a fan of Joel Osteen. His spirituality presented within an earthly message of action works for me. Life is full of challenges. I ask myself one question when I face conflict in my life or in business. Am I in Faith or am I in Fear? My faith has pulled me through some of the tougher stretches in my life. Whether your inspiration is founded in religion, spirituality or something else, I hope it is equally effective in getting you through.

I IS FOR...INDIVIDUALISM. The great Americans I admire have all been leaders, not followers: trailblazing, ahead-of-their-time visionaries who followed the beat of their own drummer. They chose the roads less followed, and we are all the beneficiaries. I have been inspired by the drive of these individuals to live life their way. May you find similar inspiration that will motivate you to achieve your dreams.

C IS FOR...CIVILITY. Cool under pressure. Always easy to get along with when the going's good. But how we respond to adversity is often what determines if we will prevail. Nobody likes to deal with a hothead. Being calm and composed within the storm of life is the way to be. Exhibit strength and composure in all your affairs. You are the boss, the leader. Nothing is going to get you down. Civility is the way.

A IS FOR…ACHIEVEMENT. Everybody loves a winner. There is nothing wrong with patting yourself on the back for some of your accomplishments. Promote yourself and your power team for the successes you are. Winners attract other winners. People love investing in winners. Establish a culture of achievement within your real estate network circle. The winning attitude is contagious. Spread it around.

N IS FOR…NOBILITY. Some of our greatest Americans exemplify nobility, class, dignity. They have enjoyed success but conduct themselves with humility. They are admired, respected, yet are so down to earth. I have done everything in my power to model myself on people like this. Wealth may come and go, but our character can never waver. A life lived with dignity has no equal.

Follow these ideals every day and I know you will realize your potential as you seek great success in all your affairs.

Epilogue

Thank you for reading my life story. By now I hope you feel informed, inspired, motivated and engaged. Thank you for trusting me and allowing me to share my story with you. My story is of course a personal one but I truly believe that, with the right tools, the right skills and the right attitude, you can achieve everything I have described in this book. My team and I are ready to join forces with you to work together in building your real estate business and portfolio.

This book with my career history started with a dream. I've come a long way from that first talk with my friend Jac. I couldn't be more proud of the wholesale real estate investing program we have developed to help you have great success. My strategies for success has been proven to work; and it can be your recipe for success if you join me today. I am proof you do not have to have money to make money.

There have been some important people in my life who have helped me, mentored me and inspired me. Some I knew personally. Others I admired from afar. Either way, I constantly aspire to their qualities. My childhood tennis coach, Nick Bollettieri and my mentor, Billie Jean King remain formative in my life even today. As a kid, I admired from afar tennis idols Jimmy Connors and Chris Evert. All of them were and are tenacious, fight-on-and-never-quit types of people. They have impacted me in a positive way. My background happens to be in sports so these were the people who most influenced my development. Your background may be different. But I am sure there are people in your life, whether known personally to you or simply people you admire, who fulfill that role for you. Look to them, and aspire to emulate their spirit, drive and determination.

So congratulations! You are ready to start out on the path to fulfilling your dreams. Just remember, my team and I are a phone call away. We are ready to coach you, to help you, to guide and inspire you. Our coaching and mentoring programs are here to support you and to help you build your success into a lifelong reality.

As we say in tennis, it's not always easy to hit the sweet spot. You'll make a few mishits. But I believe you will hit a lot of aces, too, if you use the skills in this book.

I look forward to meeting you soon. Let's go for it!

Photo by Brian Neal

Acknowledgements

My life has been one incredible journey filled with some of the most amazing people on this planet, encouraging and mentoring me along the way. From a very young age, I was encouraged to "DREAM BIG." My mother instilled in me an unshakeable faith in my potential to accomplish anything I would set my mind to. She taught me to "NEVER GIVE UP" and always push the envelope with an aggressive "GO FOR IT" attitude. Finally my mother taught me that, every day of my life, before I go to sleep at night, to thank God for the talents with which I was blessed to have been born, and to thank God for the wonderful people that have helped and inspired me to achieve many of my dreams. This is something I have done every day of my life.

Thank you, Mother.

To my first tennis coach, Jim Kelaher, who reinforced the way my mother brought me up, and for being the first person outside of my family who believed in me and was emotionally invested in my success. He taught me how to play tennis well, at which point I began to see tennis as my launching pad to a great life – a way to rise above my family's poverty.

Thank you to Hall of Fame coach Nick Bollettieri, who recognized my work ethic and talent, and provided me a tennis scholarship and new home, at his tennis academy in Bradenton, Florida when I was 15 years old. Nick's investment, time spent and love shown towards me put me on the fast track to success, and I have never looked back. I can assure you my tennis and real estate career would never have happened without Nick's role in taking charge of my life at that time.

My life was profoundly impacted once again, both personally and professionally, when I had the honor to be mentored by legendary 2009 Presidential Medal of Freedom recipient Billie Jean King. Our time together working within World Team Tennis showed me how a real winner gets things done with passion and precise execution.

These wonderful people help form the foundation for me so I could develop the confidence, along with professional and personal skill sets, to start my real estate investing career.

A huge thank you to my first real estate coach, Jac Klamper. You believed in me and gave me the real estate lesson of a lifetime in the first few years of my real estate career. Our days together will always be some of the most special times of my life. I cannot even begin to describe how excited I was to be learning from you as we turned property after property into big pay days. I love you and thank you from the heart.

Thank you to my first two financial backers on my first home project, Thomas Graham and Joe Roberts. You believed in me and saw the expertise I built with my power team in place from deal number 1.

Thank you to my multiple power teams over the years that helped me every step of the way.

I would need pages to thank everyone, but here are a few of the ones that made the biggest difference to our collective success. Anthony Ricciardo, Randy Koehnke, Travis Smith, Billy Cannon, Bill Grenier, Allen Kmiotek, Don Montgomery, Robert Sojo, Ernst Urbainczyk, Robert Gillispie, Mark Morales, Patrick Cambell, Wesley Cuyler, Jerry Kessler, Shannon Hutto, Scott Johnson, Millie Crenshaw, Jenny Tacner, Julie Coombs, Jeremy Crutchfield, Portia Rammassar, Mike Sapp, Steve Dalia, Steve Tacher, Merrill Brick, Victor Brick and Keith Collins.

A special thank you to my father, Thomas Blair, and brother, Joe Blair, who helped me in the early years tirelessly to ensure every property was renovated in the most affordable and attractive way for a future home owner. May my Dad rest in peace. I am blessed to have my brother still by my side 23 years after the very first home project I accomplished. He stands by my side every day as C.O.O. of our real estate company, Turnkey Home Buyers USA. Thank you, Joe.

Special thanks to my TBG Holdings family who recognized the market conditions in 2015 were the Perfect Storm for Real Estate Investors to reenter the market. Thanks to Timothy Hart, Sharon and Samuel Ford, and Denny DeMartin, as we worked together in pursuit of helping everybody reach their personal real estate investing goals.

Thank you, Brian Neal, for being such a tenacious and passionate Real Estate broker.

Special thanks to Jamie Forsythe, my go-to guy for things organizational, editorial and procedural. Keith Chamlee, thank you for your tireless loyalty and creativity – as well as Dennis Dean and Ed Baker, our Creative Directors, making sure we are always the best-dressed media in the business. What would I do without you guys!

Thank you to all my lenders over the years. Your trust and belief in me is so appreciated. A very special thank you to my longtime great friend and business partner Shane Hackett. You recognized something special in me as you hired me to be the national real estate investing spokesperson for *Success Magazine*. That changed my life incredibly because it allowed me to get back to what I love — being a coach to thousands of people all across the United States. I spend time with them in large and small venues to educate, encourage and mentor their pursuit of achieving success as real estate investors. Thank you Shane, as well, for a heartfelt foreword to this book. I love you very much.

Finally, thank you to all of you who read my story. My hope is we will have the opportunity to meet and spend time together, share stories and strategies working in today's market. My promise is, implement the proven business model I set out in this book, learn from the mistakes I discussed, and you will be well on your way to seeing your dreams come true.

Statement by James Forsythe

I have been a member of Bobby's Power Team since 2003. Initially I was brought on as a technology consultant, charged with automating the office and developing an electronic storage system. But, it was not long before I was thoroughly involved in all aspects of the business in order to develop programs and systems. I learned how to find properties through internet searches of the MLS and multiple real estate websites. I worked with wholesalers and the acquisition teams in locating and evaluating great home run deals. I oversaw and managed the renovation teams to ensure that properties were renovated on time and budget. I worked with the marketing team to design brochures, websites and other marketing material. And I worked closely with the back end teams to make sure documents for final sale or rental were all in order. But my greatest skill and interest was in customer service. Whether it was with the sellers, or the rehab crews, the investors or the home buyers, I was quick to listen to their concerns and questions and keep them informed.

I am proud to be a part of the Turnkey Home Buyers USA team as the Coaching coordinator. I will be there to manage our great group of coaches, making sure that they are working closely with their motivated students. I eagerly anticipate the opportunity to work with the coaches and their students to ensure that it is a great and rewarding experience for all.

As with Bobby, I am a coach and teacher at heart. To know is one thing, to understand is better. It is the difference between knowledge and wisdom. It is our goal that through our coaching and mentoring programs, that you will not just be knowledgeable investors, but wise ones. As you have read in Bobby's book, this wisdom is not just about real estate, but about our lives. Knowledge is power, Wisdom is knowing how to use it. By being wise, in real estate and in your life, you will be able to achieve your dreams.

I look forward to being a part of your Power team!

Glossary

Adjustable Rate Mortgage (ARM)	A mortgage in which the interest rate and payments are adjusted periodically during the life of the loan.
After Repair Value (ARV)	The estimated value of a property after all repairs and rehab have been completed.
Agent	A person who is authorized to act on behalf of another.
Agreement	An exchange of promises, a meeting of the minds, a mutual understanding or arrangement in contract law.
Amortization	A loan payment by equal periodic payment calculated to pay off the debt at the end of a fixed period, including accrued interest on the outstanding balance.
Appreciation	An increase in the value of the property over time.
Annual Percentage Rate (APR)	The interest rate reflecting the cost of a mortgage as a yearly rate.
Appraisal	An estimate of the value of property, made by a qualified professional called an "appraiser".
Asking Price (Listing Price)	The price that the owner or agent would like to receive for the property.
Assessment	A local tax levied against a property for a specific purpose, such as streetlights, sewer, or road improvements.
Assessed Value	The value as determined by the Property Appraiser's Office determining the value of the property for tax purposes.
Assignment	The transfer of a contract, deed or title from one person to another.
Assumption	The agreement between buyer and seller where the buyer takes over the payments on an existing mortgage from the seller.
Auction	Bidding on available properties. Can be done at local courthouses for bankruptcies or on line.
Back-Up Offer	A secondary bid for a property that the seller will accept if the first offer fails.
Balloon (Payment) Mortgage	Usually a short-term fixed-rate loan that involves small payments for a certain period of time and one large payment for the remaining amount of the principal at a time.

Bankruptcy	The inability of a debtor to pay one's financial debts when due and where relief has been sought and has been granted through a special court action that makes it possible to resolve or eliminate.
Borrower (Mortgagor)	One who applies for and receives a loan in order to purchase a home.
Building Codes	Rules and regulations established by governmental jurisdictions (City and/or County) regulating standards for new construction and renovations of properties.
Bridge Loan	A short-term loan allowing the purchaser to obtain funding for distressed property and the money to rehab. Also called "hard money".
Broker	An individual or company that assists in arranging funding, or negotiating contracts for a client. Brokers usually charge a fee or receive a commission for their services.
Cancellation Clause	A provision in a contract that gives a party the right to terminate his or her obligations upon the occurrence of specified conditions or events.
Capital Gains Tax	The taxable profit earned from the sale of a capital asset.
Cash Flow	The amount of cash a rental property investor receives after deducting operating expenses and loan payments from gross income.
Closing	The meeting between the buyer, seller and lender or their agents where the property and funds legally change hands. Also called settlement.
Closing Costs	Usually include an origination fee, discount points, appraisal fee, title search and insurance, survey, taxes, deed recording fee, credit report charge and other costs assessed at settlement. The costs of closing usually range from 3% to 6% of the mortgage amount.
Comparables	The value of similar properties in close approximation to a property used to help establish the value of a property.
Counter Offer	An offer or bid given in response to another bid or offer.
Contingency	A provision in a contract that requires a certain act to be done or an event to occur before the contract becomes binding.
Contract of Sale	A contract between the purchaser and the seller to convey title of the property.
Conventional Loan	A mortgage not insured by FHA or guaranteed by the VA.
Credit Report	A report documenting the credit history and current credit status of the borrower.
Deed-in-lieu	Gives control of the deed/title of a property back to the lender in case of default on a loan or foreclosure.
Debt-to-Income Ratio	The ratio, expressed as a percentage, which results when a borrower's monthly payment obligation on long-term debts is divided by his or her gross monthly income.
Deed of trust	In many states, this document is used in place of a mortgage to secure the payment of a note.

Default	Failure to meet legal obligations in a contract. Specifically, failure to make the monthly payments on a mortgage.
Delinquency	Failure to make payments on time.
Department of Veterans Affairs (VA)	An independent agency of the federal government which guarantees long-term, low-or no-down payment mortgages to eligible veterans.
Distressed Property	Property that is in poor physical or financial condition.
Down Payment (Deposit)	Money paid to make up the difference between the purchase price and the mortgage amount.
Draw	A payment made to subcontractors or suppliers from a construction loan.
Duplex	A dwelling having apartments with separate entrances for two households.
Earnest Money	Money given by a buyer to a seller as part of the purchase price to bind a transaction or assure payment.
Encumbrance	A claim or lien on a property which complicates the title process.
Equity	The difference between the value an owner has in real estate and the obligations against the property.
Escrow	Monies deposited with a third party to be released after conditions of the contract are met.
Estate	The total assets of a person, including real property, at the time of death.
Exclusive Listing	A contract that gives an agent the exclusive right to market a property for a specific period of time.
Fannie Mae	A corporation created by Congress that purchases and sells conventional residential mortgages as well as those insured by FHA or guaranteed by VA.
Federal Housing Administration (FHA)	A division of the Department of Housing and Urban Development. Its main activity is the insuring of residential mortgage loans made by private lenders. FHA also sets standards for underwriting mortgages
FHA Loan	A loan insured by the Federal Housing Administration open to all qualified home purchasers.
FHA Mortgage Insurance	Requires a fee (up to 2.25 percent of the loan amount) paid at closing to insure the loan with FHA. In addition, FHA mortgage insurance requires an annual fee of up to 0.5 percent of the current loan amount, paid in monthly installments.
Finder's Fee	A fee in any amount that is paid to someone for finding a property.
Fixed Rate Mortgage	The mortgage that specifies that the interest rate will remain the same throughout the term of the mortgage for the original borrower.

Fixer Upper	A house that needs refurbishment or remodeling It usually sells at a below-market price.
Forced Sale	An involuntary sale of property, usually forced by law, to pay a debt.
Foreclosure	A legal process by which the lender or the seller forces a sale of a mortgaged property because the borrower has not met the terms of the mortgage. Also known as a repossession of property.
For Sale by Owner (FSBO)	The process of a property owner selling real estate without the representation of a real estate broker or real estate agent.
Freddie Mac	A quasi-governmental agency that purchases conventional mortgage from insured depository institutions and HUD-approved mortgage bankers.
General Contractor	A general contractor is responsible for providing all of the material, labor, equipment and services necessary for the renovation of the project.
Income Property	Property that is not occupied by the owner but is used to generate income.
Individual Retirement Account (IRA)	Tax-deferred savings accounts that allow people to accrue retirement funds.
Interest Only Loan	The borrower pays only the interest that accrues on the loan balance each month. Because each payment goes toward interest, the outstanding balance of the loan does not decline with each payment.
Investment Property	Real estate that generates income, such as an apartment building or a rental house.
Landscape	A home's surroundings can range from a shrub-studded emerald lawn to a native-plant xeriscape. It is a major component of curb appeal.
Legal Description	A specific way of identifying and locating a piece of real estate that is acceptable to a court.
Lease	An agreement to rent a property between the owner and tenant for an agreed time frame and amount.
Leverage	The use of a small amount of cash--a 5 percent or 10 percent down payment--to buy a piece of property.
Licensed Contractor	A contractor who is authorized by the municipality (State/ City/ County) to perform structural work on properties.
Lien	A claim upon a piece of property for the payment or satisfaction of a debt obligation.
Lis Pendens	A written notice that a lawsuit has been filed concerning real estate. The notice is filed in the county land records office. Recording a *lis pendens* against a piece of property alerts a potential purchaser or lender that the property's title is in question, which makes the property less attractive to a buyer or lender.
Loan-to-Value Ratio	The relationship between the amount of the mortgage loan and the appraised value of the property expressed as a percentage.

Management Company	A company that handles the rental and maintenance of a property. Services performed can include finding a tenant, marketing, screening, collecting rents, performing minor maintenance and repairs.
Management Fee	The amount you pay for services provided by a management company. Usually all or half of the first month rent and up to 10% each following month.
Market Value (Fair Market Value)	The highest price that a buyer would pay and the lowest price a seller would accept on a property.
Mortgage Insurance	Money paid to insure the mortgage when the down payment is less than 20 percent.
Mortgagee	The lender.
Mortgagor	The borrower or homeowner.
Motivated Seller	Any seller with a strong incentive to make a deal.
Multiple Listing Service (MLS)	A service used by Real Estate Agents to list properties that are for sale. Listings will contain information on the property, selling agent and price. Usually restricted to real estate agents.
No-Documentation Loan	A loan application that does not require verification of income but typically is granted in cases of large down payments.
Non Assumption Clause	A statement in the contract forbidding the assumption of the mortgage without prior approval of the lender.
Offer	An agreement to purchase a property at a specified price if accepted.
Owner Financing	When the current owner of a property agrees to finance to the buyer part or all of the purchase price.
Origination Fee	The fee charged by a lender to prepare loan documents, make credit checks, inspect and sometimes appraise a property; usually computed as a percentage of the face value of the loan.
PITT	Principal. Interest, Taxes and Insurance. Also called monthly housing expense.
Points	Prepaid interest assessed at closing by the lender. Each point is equal to 1 percent of the loan amount.
Power of Attorney	A legal document authorizing one person to act on behalf of another.
Probate Sale	A real estate sale triggered by the death of the owner, with proceeds to be divided among heirs or creditors.
Purchase Agreement (Contract For Sale)	A document which details the purchase price and conditions of the transaction. Contracts for Sale are state specific.
Quad	A dwelling having apartments with separate entrances for four households.
Quit Claim Deed	A document that releases a party from any interest in a piece of real estate.

Realtor	A real estate broker or an associate holding active membership in a local real estate board affiliate with the National Association of Realtors.
Real Estate	Land and anything permanently affixed to it, including buildings, fences and other items attached to the structure.
Recission	The cancellation of a contract. With respect to mortgage refinancing, the law that gives the homeowner three days to cancel a contract in some cases once it is signed if the transaction uses equity in the home as security.
Refinance	Obtaining a new mortgage loan on a property already owned.
Rent Loss Insurance	A policy that covers any loss of rent or rental value in the event of fire or other damage that renders the property uninhabitable.
RESPA	Abbreviation for the Real Estate Settlement Procedures Act. RESPA is a federal law that allows consumers to review information on known or estimated settlement costs once after application and once prior to or at a settlement. The law requires lenders to furnish the information after application only.
Return On Investment (ROI)	The amount of profit a property generates.
Second Mortgage	A mortgage made subsequent to another mortgage and subordinate to the first mortgage.
Secured Loan	Any loan backed by collateral.
Sub-Contractor	Specialized contractors hired by a general contractor to perform all or portions of the construction work.
Stipulations	Clauses added to a contract that set conditions for the closing of the sale.
Sweat Equity	Equity created by a purchaser performing work on a property being purchased.
Survey	A measurement of land, prepared by a registered land surveyor, showing the location of the land with reference to known points, its dimensions, and the location and the location and dimensions of any buildings.
Tax Sale	The public sale of a property by the government for nonpayment of taxes.
Tenant	Person who rents a property and signs a lease agreement.
Title	A document that gives evidence of an individual's ownership of property.
Title Insurance	A policy, usually issued by a title insurance company, which insures a homebuyer against errors in the title search.
Title Search	An examination of municipal records to determine the legal ownership of property.

VA Loan	A long-term, low, or no-down payment loan guaranteed by the Department of Veterans Affairs. Restricted to individuals qualified by military service or other entitlements.
Variable Rate Mortgage (VRM)	See "Adjustable Rate Mortgage."
Verification of Deposit (VOD)	A document signed by the borrower's financial institution verifying the status and balance of his/her financial accounts.
Verification of Employment (VOE)	A document signed by the borrower's employer verifying his/her position and salary.
Waiver	A voluntary relinquishing of certain rights or claims.
Zoning	Regulations that control the use of land within a jurisdiction.